Words To Encourage
And Brighten Your Day

Judy Proffitt

ISBN: 979-8-9882302-0-5

All scriptures are taken from the King James Version (KJV): King James Version, public domain.

A Word From The Author

Therefore comfort each other and edify one another,
just as you also are doing.
1 Thessalonians 5:11

This book is a compilation of poetry written over many years. A lot of the poems have been printed and given away in various smaller books. Quite a few of them have been written in the last several years and have never been seen in print.

Inspiration for the poems I write often comes from a Pastor's sermon. Many were written to encourage special friends at various times in their lives, especially in times of suffering, hardships, or grief. Many are inspired by observing God's wonderful Creation, or by my own personal life experiences and study of God's Word.

I pray they will encourage you, perhaps make you smile, and always to think of the Goodness and Greatness of our Heavenly Father, and our Saviour, the Lord Jesus Christ.

Judy Proffitt

From The Publisher

And for me, that utterance may be given unto me,
that I may open my mouth boldly,
to make known the mystery of the gospel,
for which I am an ambassador in bonds:
that therein I may speak boldly, as I ought to speak.
Ephesians 6:19-20

Around The Corner Ministries exists to proclaim the gospel. Founded in 2016, the ministry serves to equip followers of Jesus to become bold witnesses of the grace and goodness of God. Part of our ministry is through the written word, devotionals, Bible studies, blogging, and now, a book of poetry written and compiled by Sheila's mother, Judy Proffitt.

Judy has written hundreds of poems over the years and given all of them away to bless and encourage others and testify about the eternal salvation we find in Jesus. You might run into her in the grocery store, where she will strike up a conversation and before she walks away, she has handed you a copy of the three or four poems she always carries in her purse. Inevitably it will speak to your heart at just the right time.

Judy prefers not to sell her poems. She feels they are a gift from the Lord, and she is simply a steward of them to bless others and share the gospel. All proceeds from the sale of this book will be used to continue that mission, printing more copies that can be shared as widely as possible.

We hope you enjoy the read and discover a fresh appreciation for the goodness and grace of the Lord Jesus.

Todd & Sheila Alewine
Founders, Around The Corner Ministries
aroundthecornerministries.org

TABLE OF CONTENTS

6

Walking By Faith

Fight the good fight of faith,
lay hold on eternal life, whereunto thou art also called,
and hast professed a good profession
before many witnesses.
1 Timothy 6:12

TRUST

Sometimes the place we are called to walk,
Is filled with unknown turns.
We wonder what God has in store,
What lessons we must learn.

Then we find, as days go by,
What He is trying to teach.
It is, that His Grace is all sufficient,
And we are not beyond His reach.

What lies ahead, we do not know.
But trust in Him, we must.
We will place our lives in God's strong arms,
And in Him, we will fully trust.

THE TRAPEZE

The man in the Circus on the flying trapeze,
Sails thru the air, with the greatest of ease.
But on the Trapeze of Life, sometimes we find,
We are caught in midair and suspended in time.

The breeze isn't gentle, it's a fierce stormy gale.
As we reach for the next bar, we are afraid we will fail.
From one trapeze bar to the next we seek,
It seems far away, and beyond our reach.

Will we make it across, and safely land
Or will we fall short, and it slip from our hand?
The Trapeze of Life, seems to never be still,
We are tossed to and fro, against our will.

There is no safety net, and we fear we will fall;
"Reach for the next bar," life continually calls.
No platform is permanent, we have to keep going,
The winds of change forever are blowing.

There is no turning back, once we make the first leap,
We just hope the next bar, is not beyond our reach.
When Life's Act is over, and the bar is still,
Many hopes and dreams will yet be unfulfilled.

On the final platform when we finally stand,
We will realize we always were safe in God's hand.

THE ONLY CHILD

An only child is petted, and usually quite spoiled.
They're never denied anything, their parents give them the world.
Their every wish is granted, their needs are always supplied.
They know they are very special, the apple of a parent's eye.

An only child inherits everything their parents own.
They don't have to share with anyone; all is for them alone.
God treats all of His children as if they were the only one.
He makes them joint heirs with Him; all that He has, they own.

So, every Christian is special;
God holds them in His hand.
When we say we have special privileges,
the world just can't understand.

Though treated as an only child,
We have many Sisters and Brothers,
And the special love we are shown,
Helps us to love one another.

When an only child is adopted,
A greater miracle is known;
He is chosen from countless others,
and claimed as their very own.

So, now, we cry, Abba Father.
For God has made us His own.
Not only bought with His Blood;
But adopted as daughters and sons.

THE BIRD'S CHURCH

There's a tree outside my window
Where the birds have church each day.
The limbs are pews on which they sit,
To sing their songs of praise.

Sometimes they quietly sit; it seems they are at rest.
Sometimes they flutter all about, and work to build a nest.
Sometimes there is a lot of noise, the Woodpecker has arrived,
He hammers loud and chips will fly, to find his food inside.

The tiny little Sparrow quietly hops around,
She picks up sticks and blades of grass,
To feather the nest, she's found.

Then the harmless gentle Dove
Waits to see what is on the ground,
But if the greedy Blue Jay has been there,
There is nothing to be found.

Sometimes it is like an airshow
When the pigeons all swoop down,
They fly in flocks together
And one by one, they hit the ground.

Sometimes it is like a painted canvas
With colors red and blue,
The Cardinal and the Robin,
The Finches' bright gold hue.

What a wonderful creation
God has given us to share.
We should thank Him for this beauty,
And join the birds, in song and prayer.

HELL

Hell was not created for me and you,
But for the Devil, and His fallen crew.
They dishonored God, and tried to rebel,
So, they were cast down, and reserved for Hell.

God didn't want man, His highest creation
To find Hell as their final destination.
He sent His Son, to die on the Cross,
So that all who believed, would never be lost.

Just trust in His plan of eternal salvation,
Put your faith in His Blood, for your propitiation,

He died in your stead,
And if you believe,
Repent of your sins, and His forgiveness receive.
Your home will be Heaven,
When this life you leave.

SLEEP

When nighttime falls, and it is time for rest
Why should we lie awake,
And toss and turn, and worry and fret
About the path tomorrow will take?

The Psalmist said, "I will lay down in peace,
I will not be afraid, but sleep.
For the God who kept me all through the day,
I will trust to safely keep."

We can sleep as a babe in his mother's arms,
Who knows no fear and feels no harm.
He goes to sleep peacefully, with a contented sigh,
Assured she will respond to his weakest cry.

Our Heavenly Father, neither slumbers nor sleeps.
He guides through the day, and the night watch He keeps.
We can rest in His care without any fear;
Knowing He has promised to always be near.

Sleep is the healer of the cares of life,
We waken refreshed, to begin a new day.
So, cradle your head on a pillow of Trust,
Knowing God cares, and will keep your way.

THE PASTOR

Have you ever gone to church when it was not a scheduled day,
Just sat quietly in the pew, to meditate, and pray?
As you looked around you at all the empty pews,
The silence there was awesome, no one there but God, and you.

When you leave the Sanctuary, and quietly close the door,
You know you've been to church,
but you feel there should be more.

Then if you went to Sunday School
And heard someone, the lesson teach,
But in the Worship Hour, no one was there to preach.
You heard the organ music, and prayers were offered up;
Everything was beautiful, the choir sang, just enough.

But when you leave, you know something was not there
God's Word was not proclaimed, for the pulpit still was bare.
God loves it when we worship, and loves the Bible teaching,
But His method of the Gospel, is through foolishness of preaching.

The preaching of the Word inspired, is how He brings conviction,
For nothing can replace, the power wrought through Scripture.
The Pastor is a mortal man, the same as me and you,
But God placed him as His spokesman,
To instruct us in the pew.

It's beyond our comprehension,
That God would use a mortal man.
And anoint him with His Spirit,
To preach Salvation's plan.

TRUE FORGIVENESS

When someone asks for forgiveness
For a wrong, or a hurt, they have caused.
We are quick to say, "I forgive you"
Without a hesitant pause.

But each time we see the offender,
The first thing that comes to our mind,
Is the pain we felt, at the wrong they did,
When they were being unkind.

Then feelings rise up, and we are unsure
Did we really want to forgive
And clear their conscience, and so easily accept
The apology they offered to give?

But our Heavenly Father holds no such thoughts,
When we truly repent of our sins.
He puts them under the Blood, and blots them out,
To be never mentioned again.

He cast them into the Sea of Forgetfulness
And when we begin to doubt,
God says, "So deep in the Sea, your sins I have cast,
What sins are you talking about?"

How deep is this Sea of Forgetfulness?
It is as deep, as the East is far from the West.
As we forgive others, He forgives our debts.
But only the God of all Grace,
Can forgive and forget.

EARTHEN VESSELS

We are to lay up treasures in Heaven
Where they will be safe and secure.
For earthly possessions are useless,
And nothing down here, will endure.

But God sent Heaven's prized Treasure
To Earth, wrapped in human form.
The flesh that will always be temporal,
Housed our Saviour before He was born.

In these frail, broken vessels
God placed His Treasure so rare.
He left all the splendor of Heaven
Our sins and infirmities to bear.

It is hard to conceive that such Treasure,
God put in these vessels of dust,
To think that His Plan of Salvation,
In such frailty He would entrust.

We are to be vessels of honor
Made fit for the Master's use.
Though broken, and frail, and earthly,
He imparts the Word of His Truth.

He chooses to use such vessels
Yet He knows we are made of clay.
He allows us to share His great message,
That He is the Truth, and the Way.

DRESSED FOR THE JOURNEY
Colossians 3

As we make our journey Heavenward to the beautiful city so fair.
We must dress for the trip, in the proper attire,
And these are what we should wear.

Our shoes are MERCY and KINDNESS
Treating our fellow man with Christian love,
To set the example, so they will see, our sights are set on above.

We must think not too highly of our own regard,
But willing a Servant to be.
We must wear HUMILITY, as our daily dress,
And spend much time on our knees.

Our clothes of MEEKNESS, must be daily worn,
And cast off pride as a rag,
Exalting others before ourselves;
Of our own works, never to brag.

An apron of PATIENCE will protection provide
From hasty remarks, and revenge.
We will find helping others will bless our lives,
And keep us from bitterness clean.

The everyday garment we should wear the most
Should the gown of FORGIVENESS be.
When we are wronged, and offended by man,
From grudges and hate, we'll be free.

To keep all these garments and virtues in place
We have one more garment to don.
The ROBE OF LOVE, tied with the cords of Grace
Is the most important of all that we own.

GOD REMEMBERS

When God closed the door on Noah in the Ark,
He didn't forget he was there.
Noah didn't know what lie ahead,
But he knew he was in God's care.

The only window was placed on top,
And the Ark was dark and drear.
God didn't send a sign, or speak a word to Noah,
In the space of more than a year.

Noah must have wondered about the world outside,
And he must have had times of doubt.
But he assured himself, that if God closed him in.
Then God would lead him out.

As the days wore on, Noah must have thought,
"How long do we stay in here?
With the walls closing in, and the animal smells,
And not a ray of cheer?"

When he would doubt, he would tell himself,
"I can't tell the day from the night.
But I will still remember, in this time of darkness,
How God spoke to me in the light."

So, when you feel the walls closing in,
And your heart is filled with fear,
Remember Noah, whom God didn't forget,
His watchful eye is near.

Then the day came, when God opened the door,
And Noah saw a world that was new.
And the first thing he saw, when he came outside.
Was a beautiful Rainbow in view.

God told Noah, "This rainbow you see,
Is a promise that I still care.
You can rest assured whatever befalls,
My presence will always be there."

So, we, as Noah, adrift on the Sea of Life,
With waves of sorrow swelling high.
The God who kept Noah safe in the Ark,
Will answer our heart's weakest cry.

Noah didn't see the Rainbow while still in the Ark,
He had to wait till the rains were through.
You will find, as Noah, after all of life's storms,
The Rainbow still proves,
God's promises are true.

THE REMNANT

It was ragged and torn, and starting to fray;
Just a small scrap of cloth, someone threw away.
Cast out in the refuse, no use could be seen,
It was too small to matter, and was soiled, and unclean.

Just a remnant of cloth, why bother to keep?
Let it fall where it may, till the broom makes its sweep.
But One came along, with an artistic eye,
Saw the remnant as useful, loved the weave, and the dye.

This piece will be perfect in the quilt I will make,
It is just the right color, and just the right shape.
I'll trim it, and seam it, and wash it so clean;
A more beautiful quilt has not yet been seen.

The small remnant that seemed so worthless and cheap,
Was just the right one the quilt maker would keep.
So, we, who are ragged, and frayed, and cast down,
May be just what is needed for the Bride's Wedding Gown.

For His strength is made perfect in our flesh that is weak.
He takes our frayed remnants and makes them complete.
In His Master Design, for His Quilt of Great Grace;
Our small remnants, we'll find, will all have a place.

ROMANS 12:1

The Spirit is willing, but the flesh is weak,
And we fail so often, when His will we seek.
We want to give our souls to Him,
But we let the fire of sacrifice, burn so dim.

As the priest took the flesh hooks, and controlled the lamb,
So, He guides us, and keeps us, in the palm of His hand.
If we are willing to sacrifice all,
He will lead us, and keep us, if on Him, we call.

The sacrifice we make is a daily event
As we enter to worship, where the veil was rent.
For we can come boldly to take our place,
And offer ourselves, to His Throne of Grace.

The priest stood ready, with the flesh hooks close by,
If the sacrifice slipped, or the fire started to die.
He would bring back the offering, keep it under the flame,
For the sacrifice to be accepted, and remove sin's shame.

Sometimes, when we think we are where we should be,
God, in His mercy, will cause us to see.
That we must surrender to His hooks in our soul,
As He guides us, and leads us, to Heaven, our goal.

We have nothing to offer, our righteousness fails,
We could never be worthy to go beyond the veil.
But the priest of our souls, Jesus the Son,
Makes us accepted by God,
For in Him, we are One.

A LETTER FROM JAMES

James' letter to the Churches gives us much to think about,
And when we see ourselves, it is not a time to shout.
In Chapter number One, He tells us we are frail.
And if we do not look to God, in temptations, we will fail.

Undefiled religion is keeping God's commands.
When looking in the mirror of His Word,
We ask for strength and wisdom, to firmly take a stand.
He promised us a crown of life, if we will keep His Way,
He is Jesus Christ, always the same, today, and yesterday.

In James Chapter Two, we find it is not our works,
But faith in Him who keeps us, so our duties we won't shirk.
We find all men are equal, and no favorites we must play,
Or when He comes to judge our works,
They will burn as stubble, wood, and hay.

Our works must come from faith in Him, and Him alone,
Then when we do for others, our love for Christ is known.
We learn from James our hearts are filled with much deceit;
When we recognize Earth's famous, and offer the best seat.

We must not regard man's honor, or his station in this life,
For all men stand on equal ground,
Beneath the Cross of Jesus Christ.

We learn about our tongue, it is most difficult to tame,
This is taught so clearly, in Chapter Three of James.
In our tongue we have much power, we can either curse or bless
But the conversation of the Peaceful,
Bears the fruit of righteousness.

Our tongue is like an untamed beast that can easily run away.
So daily we must ask God's keeping for these mortal lips of clay.
He gave us lips to guard our tongues, so we would not let it slip,
For our tongue controls our destiny, like the rudder on a ship.

So daily let us ask Him, to help us say what is worthwhile
To give us Grace to keep our tongue,
And our lips from speaking guile.

Chapter Four of James, tells us we can serve only One in life
For we will either walk in worldly ways,
Or strive to please our Christ.
For if we love this world, James tells us very plain,
We are the enemies of God, and bring dishonor to His Name.

He will give us Grace to serve Him, if we show humility
But He resists the proud and boastful,
His disciples, they cannot be.
If we resist the Devil, God said that he would flee,
And we'll find our walk with Jesus, much sweeter it will be.

Then James closes out his letter when he writes in Chapter Five
He tells us with patience in our hearts, we will truly be alive.
He tells us to stay humble, and if another we offend,
We must quickly confess it, and our brother we will win.

The reason for James' letter
Is found in verse eight of Chapter Five.
To keep our hearts established,
For Christ's Coming draweth nigh.

FAITH

We walk by faith, and not by sight;
Peter found this to be true.
For he found he failed to completely trust,
When Jesus was plainly in view.

When Jesus walked on the water, and told Peter, he could too,
He thought he could trust, but then he found,
His fears, and his doubts, let him down.

Just an arm's length away from the Saviour's help.
Close enough to see His face.
Yet when Peter tried to prove he believed,
He found, he didn't have faith.

He knew who bid him to walk that day,
He knew that CHRIST WAS LORD.
Yet his faith was weak, and he looked to himself,
And stood not on Christ's Word.

So today, we find it hard to trust,
And hard to really have faith,
We know we believe that His Word is true,
And we know we can lean on His Grace.

But we, as Peter, are human and weak,
And lean on Him we must.
Our nature rebels, and fills us with doubt,
When we try so hard to trust.

He that comes to God, must believe that HE IS,
And must trust with heart and soul.
We must learn that we cannot make it alone,
It is HIS FAITH, that makes us whole.

HEAVEN'S STORE HOUSE

There is a Store House of Blessings in Heaven,
Where the doors open without a key.
Prayer is the secret that opens,
When we spend time on our knees.

God delights in blessing His children,
He stands ready His gifts to bestow.
When in faith we kneel before Him,
And walk in the path that He shows.

There is a special blessing
Reserved for those of His Own.
For He grants to them, the privilege,
To come boldly before His Throne.

His ears are ever attentive
To the Righteous one's fervent cry.
When they ask, not amiss, but humbly,
Their needs, He will gladly supply.

THE MASTER ARTIST

The Master Artist in Heaven
Is painting beautiful scenes,
They are on display for the Angels,
To see the works of the Redeemed.

The angels know not of Redemption,
They dwell in the Heavens above.
They have no part of Salvation,
They are not Saved by His Blood.

They are created beings, and angels,
They worship, and honor, and praise,
But they can never sing of Redemption,
They had no need to be saved.

But on this canvas in Heaven,
God displays the works of His Own,
The Angels, and created beings,
Stand in awe, at what they are shown.

Our works should be for His Glory,
All that we do, bring Him praise.
Our motive is only to please Him,
And serve Him, all of our days.

HATRED

Why do people let those they hate
Live inside their head?
They hate everything about them,
And even wish them dead.

Their anger rises up
When they hear the person's name
But the person that is hated,
Isn't playing in this game.

They don't know how much you hate them,
And if they did, they wouldn't care.
They go on about their business,
Of you, they aren't aware.

So, when you spend your time in hating,
And your anger boils and stews,
You aren't hurting those you hate,
You are only hurting YOU.

If you think that someone is worthless
Don't let them control your mind.
They don't even know you hate them,
So, you are wasting all your time.

You are making them important
Of your mind, they are in charge.
The space they are occupying,
In your mind, is very large.

ARMS

When we think of the parts of the body
Our arms are first in mind.
Everything we do, depends on them, we find.
We use our arms to cuddle a child,
To do all that life demands.
Without the use of our arms,
There would be need to have hands.

When life is hard, and we are hurt and afraid;
We run to the arms of a friend.
And if trouble is headed our way,
We know those arms will defend.

We speak of arms, as a weapon to fight,
To protect ourselves, to bear arms, is our right.
But the arms we need
Are the arms that hold us with love,
Though friends may help, our surest help,
Comes from God's Arms, from above.

We know the arm of flesh will fail.
Even when arms are strong.
When we try and fail, and face defeat
We need His Everlasting Arms underneath.

When trouble comes, we run to His arms,
And find what He said is true.
His left arm will embrace with love divine.
And His right arm will fight for you.

NOAH AND THE ARK

When Noah was building the ARK,
The neighbors all stood around,
They whispered and laughed to each other,
"Old Noah's mind isn't sound."

They didn't know what he was building,
They had never heard of a boat.
There was no water around them,
They knew not, of something that floats.

They said, "Noah, what are you making,
And why are you building so large?"
Noah just smiled, and said,
"Don't ask me, I'm just following God's charge."

They said, "You are overstepping your boundary,
You're not staying on your own land,
If you think we will help you move it,
We are not lending a hand."

As Noah kept building,
He told them they better heed,
For this shelter he was providing,
They soon would find, they would need.

Some watching, just stood there,
Others soon walked away,
They thought Noah had completely lost it,
They said, "What is a rainy day?"

A few decided to listen,
Said, "Maybe what he is saying is true,
But we don't understand how water can fall
From a sky that is perfectly blue."

They said, "Let's come back later,
And maybe we can see inside,
For if a big storm is coming,
It's true, there is room to hide."

But when the ark was finished,
And Noah began to look around.
None of the scoffers and neighbors,
Were anywhere to be found.

He was anxious to tell them
Now is the time to come in,
For Judgment is ready to fall,
On this evil world of sin.

But none of his friends were present,
When Noah heard God inside,
Saying, "Noah, come bring your family,
It is now the time to hide."

Noah had to be wondering,
"Is the rain really going to fall?
Am I crazy, as thought the neighbors,
Or did I really hear God's call?"

But when the blue sky clouded,
And the rain really poured down.
The neighbors came running and screaming,
"Noah, please, don't let us drown."

For forty days and nights, the sky stayed dark,
Not a ray of light.
Noah and his family were safe inside,
Experiencing a very large boat ride.

One day the ark stopped, all was still.
They were at the top of a very large hill.
Noah said to his wife, "Will you look at that,
We are on the top of Mt. Ararat."

Many days passed before they came out,
And Noah was so happy he gave a loud shout.
He said, "Looks like everything is made brand new,
And look at that beautiful RAINBOW in view."

Another Mountain held an ARK one day,
Mount Golgotha, where Jesus would pray.
"Father, forgive these men of their sin,"
In this ARK OF SALVATION, may they enter in.

The Door of Salvation stands open today,
If men repent of their sin, and for forgiveness they pray.
But like Noah's ARK, men have to choose.
Will they receive life, or Salvation, lose?

Today, God's arms of Mercy are open wide,
Like the door of the ARK, all are welcome inside.
Eternity in Heaven, is offered to all.
If you hear His Voice, you must answer His call.

TRUTH

America has decided She is in charge of herself.
She has placed God, and the Bible, away on the shelf.
We now have intelligence in our schools,
We don't need the Bible, with its old-fashioned rules.

We riot in the streets, we rob, and we kill.
We say we have freedom to do as we will.
Just because God says it, doesn't make it so;
We are intelligent enough, to decide how to go.

The Bible is old-fashioned, we've learned better now.
Yet, through it all, God is merciful somehow.
We defy His laws, shake our fists in His face,
But He still holds open, the Door of His Grace.

One way to Heaven, is too narrow minded.
Many doors open, we just need to find them.
To say that JESUS IS THE ONLY WAY
Is too old-fashioned; we know more today.

Our professors and teachers have enlightened our minds,
So many philosophies and facts, we can find.
We are smarter now, than the old folks of yore.
Higher education has opened new doors.

But man left to himself, is only a fool.
He thinks only what matters, is taught by the school.
Education has damned a whole generation,
For this life only, have they made preparation.

But GOD WILL RULE at the end of the day,
Only HIS WORD will have the final say.
AT THE NAME OF JESUS, all men will kneel.
And realize then, GOD'S TRUTH IS FOR REAL.

A LISTENING HEART

Do you have a heart that is listening?
Do you have a heart that cares?
Do you have a heart filled with love?
Do you have a heart that shares?

We speak of the "heart of the matter"
What we think of the real intent,
The reason, the motive, the final outcome,
Of what our actions have meant.

Out of the heart, the mouth speaketh,
And sometimes we are made aware;
By the things we say, that can reveal,
The thoughts that are really there.

Create in me a clean heart,
And renew a right spirit within,
Should be our daily prayer,
If our desire is others to win.

The world looks on the outward,
And our actions are all they can see.
We must ask God, to keep our hearts clean,
So, His love in us, can be seen.

YOU AIN'T SUPPOSED TO FAINT!

If life is like a treadmill
Not going anywhere,
You want to fight the enemy,
But you are only beating air.

Remember this, you are God's Saint,
And you ain't supposed to faint.
He has brought you safe this far,
And commanded you to march,
A Christian soldier is who you are.

You are told not to faint
But to stand fast, is your goal.
He permits you to "come apart"
To refresh and renew your soul.

He will lead you to green pastures
Where He allows you to sit,
But soon you have to stand again,
For you can never quit.

You are not supposed to faint,
But march ahead in Jesus' might,
You will be glad when life is over,
That you stayed faithful in the fight.

ANCHORED DEEP

The apple tree stood straight and tall,
Never thought that it would fall.
But the storm came thru, and the lightening hit,
And off the side of the tree, a large limb split.
Still the tree held its own
For deep in the ground, its roots had grown.

A year went by, and the old tree stood
Strong and sturdy as an apple tree should.
But the winds waged strong, and the snow poured down,
The tree toppled over, and lay on the ground.

But when Springtime came, the leaves turned green,
Though the tree was flat, it didn't just lean.
If you wonder how the tree had life
When the storm felled the tree like a woodsman's knife,
Though the tree had fallen and was laying down,
The roots of the tree were still in the ground.

We are like that tree when we stumble and fall,
We think we will never be any good at all.
But, like the tree, if we are planted deep,
We find we are anchored for God to keep.

If you feel you have fallen and are bearing no fruit,
Just hold to the promise that you know is truth.
If in life's storms, you fear you will fall,
Keep your roots anchored deep,
And in Him, you'll stand tall.

WE ALL ARE CALLED

We all are required to obey God's command
To give the Gospel message to every foreign land,
To send Salvation's message to the ends of the Earth,
Of Mercy, and Redemption, wrought thru the Virgin Birth.

We can't all go to the far away Nations,
To tell the lost of God's Plan of Salvation,
But we can all share in this mighty task,
To be willing to go, is all that God asks.

If just a cup of water, He places in your hands
Then just a cup of water, is all He will demand.
One waters the seed another has sown,
God gives the increase,
When His message is made known.

Those who give with a willing heart
In this Great Commission, we all have a part.
Though we can't all go, to give Salvation's Plan.
We will be glad we did our part,
When before God we stand.

MY BIBLE

My Bible is a special book,
I keep it on the shelf.
My Pastor reads from it each Sunday,
I don't have to read it for myself.

He tells me every Sunday,
How to live my life all week,
So, I leave my Bible on the shelf,
For God's instructions, I don't have to seek.

I have enough to do,
My hands are always busy,
When would I have time to read?
My days are in a tizzy.

But one day, I thought,
What if I could not hear,
Or if I could not go to church
To hear the message clear.

So, I guess it would be wise
To take my Bible off the shelf,
And let God's Word speak to my heart,
For I have to answer for myself.

AMERICA

AMERICA, once the LAND OF DREAMS,
Now is falling apart at the seams.
Once our trust in God was placed.
Now we are stooped in shame and disgrace.

Once in the World, we stood so tall,
Now the world watches as we fall.
Once we had Statesmen to lead our Nation
Now we have leaders that support degradation.

Once our school days started over the intercom
A prayer for the day, and a verse from the Psalms.
Now we have drills to "shelter" or "run"
From the angry student brandishing a gun.

Once we celebrated joy and life,
Now the unborn faces the abortionist's knife.
Once we took pride in working for our living
Now we depend on the Government giving.

Once our leaders worked to keep our land free,
Now they seek office, saying, "What's in it for me?"
They enact laws to take our freedom away,
Caring only about having their way.

It's an insult to God, to ask Him to Bless
When our lives, and our Country is in such a mess.
We can't ask for Blessing, but for Mercy we cry;
Please God, intervene, don't let America die.

CROSSROADS

One day I came to the Crossroads
And I had a decision to make.
Those who followed around me,
Watched to see which I would take.

One way was well lit with sunshine;
The Road was wide and smooth.
The other was dark, steep, and winding,
And I was left to choose.

Should I take the wide road,
And hope it wouldn't become a dead end?
Or go to the road with the challenge,
And see what's behind all the bends?

The ones with me surely would follow
The path that I chose to take,
So, I must be ever so cautious,
For they would reap my mistakes.

The Bible is true, when it says,
"No man lives or dies to himself."
So, when we come to the crossroads in life,
We should pray for God's guidance and help.

I AM NOT A WEED

Jesus was the Sower, who went forth to sow the seed,
If I belong to Him, then I am not a weed.
There are wheat and tares together
In this field of life we lead.
I may be just a small grain of wheat,
But I am not a weed.

The tares may grow around me
Which is which, is known by God.
Sometimes we cannot distinguish,
For we are made of sod.

But God knows the wheat by name
And they follow as He leads,
If I know Him by His voice,
Then I am not a weed.

When the Harvest Time is over,
And the fields of life are gleaned,
The separation will begin,
And we'll see the Blood-washed clean.

The tares will burn forever
For they are the Devil's seed,
But I will live with God in Heaven,
Because I am not a weed.

THE INNER BEAUTY

Man looks on the outward appearance,
But God looks on the whole,
The real beauty of a person
Is found within the soul.

A person may have beauty beyond compare,
They may be blessed with beauty that is rare,
But if the soul is barren and void of love and care,
If the inner man is lacking, then it matters not, how fair.

It takes a lot of living to produce an inward beauty.
Sometimes it takes sorrow, and a life of duty.
Hardship and pain, and loneliness too,
Is sometimes required, for the beauty to come thru.

A face lined with suffering is sometimes the most fair;
And the most beautiful person, is the one bowed with care.
Life sometimes is cruel, and the battles so real;
When the Potter of life puts us on the wheel.

A face that is radiant and beams with grace,
Belongs to the one with the most sorrow to face.
The smiles that help us as we go on our way;
Belong to the ones, who most dearly pay.

The inner beauty of a person is plain to see,
Shines from the soul, that submissive will be;
As we bow to His plan, and submit to His will.
We find that our life with true beauty is filled.

OUR HELP IS IN THE ROCK OF AGES

Life's Road is stony, and rough, and steep
But the "Rock of Ages" our way will keep.
The rocks of life can become stones of His Grace;
On which we climb, till we see His face.

When the rocks of life make us stumble and fall;
To the blessed Rock of Ages, we quickly call.
He puts us up, upon the Rock of Grace,
Where we rest secure in the light of His face.

When the way is difficult and hard to face,
Then He fills our path with sufficient Grace.
On the Rock of Salvation, He lets us stand,
Safe and secure, from life's sinking sand.

As the Psalmist of old, we can know first-hand
How He lifts us up, and makes us to stand.
From earth's miry pit, and crumbling clay,
He anchors us deep,
In The Rock to stay.

I'LL JUST GO ON ANYWAY

When the Devil would tell you,
No one cares, and you've had a bad day.
Just tell him to mind his own business,
And you've decided to go on anyway.

When no one stops to commend you
When you've worked so hard all day.
Just say, "It really doesn't matter,
I'll just go on anyway."

When you try to help your neighbor
And you've labored and toiled all day,
When the Devil says, "He isn't grateful,"
Just say, "I'll go on anyway."

When you go the second mile for your brother,
And you know he won't offer to pay,
Just say, "I did it for Jesus,
And I'll just go on anyway."

When you preach, or you teach, or you witness
And the world no attention will pay,
Don't give up, or quit trying,
Just say, "I'll go on anyway."

If the world won't stop to hear you,
If they tell you to be on your way;
If they turn a deaf ear to your message,
Just say, "I'll go on anyway."

Then when your life here is finished,
And you've come to the end of the day.
When Heaven is beckoning you welcome.
You will be glad, you went on anyway.

FLOWERS OF PROMISES

The flowers of God's promises
Are in the Bible everywhere,
But pick them with ease
And handle them with care.

Don't crush them, or distort their meaning
But take the full promise, and leave no gleaning.
There are daisies, and roses, and promises of life,
You can take time to pick them, amid the toil and strife.

If you humble yourself to bend down low.
In the deepest valley is where the lilies grow.
There are enough promise filled flowers
To make a large bouquet
That will make a nice centerpiece
For the hearts of men today.

Pick the promise that you need from a large array.
It will make your path grow brighter,
As you walk from day to day.

Be careful with the flower that holds a promise so dear
Hold it gently, and to your heart, keep it near.
Its fragrance will fill a heart open wide,
These flowers are yours, if in Him you abide.

LIFE'S ROCKY ROAD

Some say their education is the school of hard knocks
Where life is filled with sorrow, and their path, full of rocks.
But remember as you go along,
If the rocks were removed, the brook would lose its song.

Some say rocks are obstacles on which we climb
To reach the land of sunshine, and sweet bliss sublime.
A house built on rocks, has a foundation strong.
But a rocky travelled road seems twice as long.

If we go down life's way on a road paved and smooth
We go through quickly, for there are no rocks to remove.
But when we bend low, to clear the paths of stones,
We find when we stand, we have much stronger grown.

We all want to go the road that is smooth and clean
With no rocks to pick up, and no weeds to be gleaned.
For it is back breaking work to clear a place of stones,
And most of the time, a job to be done alone.

Life's rocks are varied with size and shape
Some are disappointment, some are heartache.
There is sickness, bereavement, loneliness, and pain.
And it seems a path we travel, again, and again.

But there is another ROCK which has nothing to fear
A Rock that's always welcome and we love to have near.
It is the sweet Rock of Ages, that says "Come to Me and rest."
On this Rock you never stumble, but will always be blest.

So, if your path seems stony, and your way filled with pain;
Go to the ROCK OF AGES, and sing the great refrain;
Rock of Ages, cleft for me, let me hide myself in thee;
And take me to that Land, that is pain and trouble free.

OUR PATTERN

Would you want to know what is expected of you,
Just ask yourself, "What would Jesus do?"
When you are faced with decisions to make,
Just ask yourself, "Which way Jesus would take?"

He is our pattern for daily living,
He is our example for loving and giving.
He loved the unlovable, He cared for the lost,
He gave all He had, never counting the cost.

When you are "done wrong" and not treated fair,
Put the smile on your face that Jesus would wear.
He is our example, our pattern, our rule.
He helps us in conflicts to pray and stay cool.

If we planned our lives, the pattern we'd choose,
Would be easy to go by, and easy to use
We'd leave out the places that are dark and dim,
But we must remember, our pattern is Him.

Sometimes our lives are far from carefree
That is when Jesus, says, "Come unto me.
My yoke is easy, my burden is light,
Stay close to Me, and you'll be all right."

To make something by a pattern, it has to yield
And be molded all around by the designer's will.
The Master Designer has a pattern for each,
With lessons in life, He desires to teach.

If we conform to the mold and the pattern He gives
We will find our lives much easier to live.
We are not to live for ourselves alone;
For there's a special work that is to be done.

Patterns are different in sizes and shape
And in this walk, we all have a place.
The pattern for your life would not fit me,
And you would not be happy with His design for me.

When He comes for His Church, as a Bride adorned
Will He find us ready, to His image conformed?
He said, when we saw Him, we could look on His face,
For He fashioned us like Him,
With His pattern of Grace.

A CUP OF WATER

If just a cup of water, I place within your hand
Then just a cup of water is all that I demand.
These words we often hear in regard to serving the Lord,
But do we understand the meaning of the word?

Jesus said if we would give so much as a cup of water
In the name of the Lord,
We would in no wise, lose our reward.
The reward comes not for the water, but for the attitude;
Did we give it out of love, or to seek man's gratitude?

If He gives us sunshine, He demands cheer,
If He gives suffering, He demands no fear.
If He gives health, He demands service in living,
If He gives wealth, He demands sacrifice in giving.

Whatever blessings on our life He chooses to bestow;
He expects us in return, our love for Him to show.
No fear or threat, or pay, can make us serve the Lord,
But if we love Him, we are quick to obey His Word.

Jesus said, if ye love Me, do the things that I command
And if just a cup of water I place within your hand
Then don't lose it, or be careless, for in the final hour;
Just a cup of water is all I will require.

THE SHEPHERD'S CARE

If we would enjoy the pastures of green,
If we would be refreshed by the cool still stream;
If we would be restored by the Shepherd's care,
Then we have to be willing, His voice to hear.

He can't make us lie, if we refused to submit
He can't lead us onward, if we choose to quit.
His restoration, His love, and provisions so grand.
Depend on our holding the Great Shepherd's hand.

With the oil of gladness, He will anoint our head,
A table He will set, with provisions He will spread.
Goodness and Mercy will be our guide;
If we follow the Shepherd and stay by His side.

An obedient sheep is the Shepherd's delight
He feeds it by day and protects it by night.
A sheep that will listen, and not go astray;
Will be ever listening, and quick to obey.

The Shepherd's voice the sheep hear and know
They follow Him gladly wherever He goes.
They know they can trust their lives to His care,
Close to His side, from danger they are spared.

At the end of the day and it's time to go home
They hear the Shepherd's voice, bidding them come.
With watchful eye He sees they are safe.
For they enter the sheepfold, thru Him, who is The Gate.

ON THE POTTER'S WHEEL

There's a purpose in the pressing of the molding of the clay,
When the potter at the wheel takes control and has his way.
In the kneading of the clay, it would seem to be abuse;
The potter has to use much pressure to prepare the clay for use.

Sometimes the clay is dusty and dried from long neglect;
And it must be wet with many tears to mold and to perfect.
Sometimes the clay seems worthless, and has an ugly hue;
The potter knows what it will take, for the beauty to come thru.

There are many things of beauty just waiting to be found
That are hid away in darkness, still in clay within the ground.
But the clay the potter uses is chosen with much care;
And when he puts it on the wheel, he knows what it can bear.

The kneading of the clay before it's on the wheel
Is such a painful process, and the clay must learn to yield.
The potter must be faithful, or he would give up on the clay
But he knows the end result, if he's allowed to have his way.

So, when it seems that you are worthless,
And your life counts but for naught,
Remember, worthless clay is formed
Into priceless works of art.

Our mortal lives are nothing more
Than earthly dust and clay,
But they will be vessels fit for the Master's use,
If we let Him have His way.

ACCEPTED IN HIM

Accepted in Him, what a glorious thought
Accepted because, with His blood we are bought.
His Grace has made us accepted and free,
What a wonder, He so loved you and me.

Accepted, made fit for the Master's use
Chosen in Him, what a wonderful truth.
We who were low and vile and unclean,
His blood has cleansed, and made pure within.

We were outcasts from Grace and filled with fear,
But with His blood, He has brought us near.
His Grace has made us accepted in the Beloved.
Cleansed us, purified, and glorified for above.

Man was unfit for God to accept
Until the splendor of Heaven, Jesus left.
He took on Himself our sins and uncleanness
And made us accepted in His righteousness.

When before God we stand at the Judgment Seat
When His awesome Holiness we have to meet.
We will have no merit, to look on His face,
But we will hear Him say, "Accepted through Grace."

THE GIFT OF LAUGHTER

The wonderful gift of laughter is a special one God imparts,
For He tells us in His Word, the worth of a merry heart.
A merry heart is like a balm, that helps us in life's woes.
Sometimes when we are so burdened,
A good laugh seems to help us so.

The Psalmist said, "With laughter, he fills my mouth,
And my tongue, with singing is filled,
I sing His praise, and I am made to shout,
For my heart is happy and thrilled."

There is a laughter that sometimes hurts,
When cruel jokes are played,
When we try and fail, and seem to feel that fun of us, is made.
Sometimes we laugh to keep our tears hidden from other's view,
For we know the world doesn't understand,
Only God will see us through.

Sometimes we cry, and our hearts are torn,
With sickness, and sorrows, and grief.
And we think the sun will never shine,
And we feel so helpless and weak.

But even when the tears are there, and the sleepless nights we face,
Deep within our soul still smiles, as we think of His marvelous Grace.

So, laugh when you can, it will do you good; it's medicine for the soul.
You will find, when you laugh, and rejoice aloud,
That His Joy, will make you whole.

We laugh, not as the world,
At things that are crude and wrong,
We laugh in the Lord, and our hearts rejoice,
As we praise Him in laughter and song.

THE EMMAUS ROAD

Is our walk in life, on the Emmaus Road
Walking for self, carrying our load.
Unaware that Jesus is walking along?
We think that He is just one of the throng.

Our hearts are sometimes angry, and sad,
We go on our way, with a spirit that is mad.
We don't understand why our life is so bare,
Why we have so many disappointments and cares.

We go on our way, taking life in a stride,
Unaware that Jesus is close by our side.
His comfort and help are so close and so near,
We don't even realize that it is Jesus, so dear.

Our hearts are dull and slow to believe,
Even though by faith, Salvation we have received.
In our daily walk, we stumble and fall;
When right by our side, Jesus waits for our call.

If our eyes could be opened, our hearts made to learn,
That Jesus is here, then would our hearts burn.
The light of His presence would brighten our days,
And we'd leave Emmaus and walk in His ways.

Our map is the Scripture, the Bible, our guide,
Our way is enlightened, no more wanting to hide.
When we let Him walk before, and not beside,
As we follow His footsteps, Our Faithful Guide.

RELIGHT OUR CANDLE, LORD

If we walk with the lord, in the light of His Word,
Then He promises to light our way.
He gave His Word, as a lamp for our feet,
And to light our path, all our days.
He said He is the Way, the Truth, and the Life,
If we follow, He promises, no darkness of night.
But sometimes we stray from the light that He gives,
And we choose our own places to walk, and to live.

And so, our light flickers, and there's scarcely a flame,
There seems total darkness, till we call on His Name.
We beg for forgiveness, for His light to return,
We promise always, to see that it burns.
But we are human, and our frames so frail,
And over and over, we stumble and fail.

The darkness of night seems to hide His face,
Till each time we pray for the light of His Grace.
It doesn't take much to extinguish the flame,
The hurts caused by others sometimes is to blame.
When our spirits are wounded, and we're made to doubt.
If we are not careful, the fire will go out.
We must shield our candle from the winds that blow,
The winds of sickness, sorrow, and things that hurt so.

May the globe of His love, keep our flame burning bright,
So, we may light the way, for some soul who needs light.
We are like candles which have to be lit,
With no power of its own, the flame easily quits.
The least movement of wind, or breeze of the air,
Causes the flame to die and disappear.
So, we ask the Lord Jesus who is light and life,
To keep us burning thru this darkness and strife.
May those of the world see the light of His face,
Relight our candle, Lord, so we portray Your Grace.

THE YOUNG LAD'S LESSON

There is a lesson we can learn from the little lad,
Who shared his loaves and fishes, giving all the lunch he had.
When Jesus seated the thousands upon the grass so green;
The little lad, who gave his lunch, was nowhere to be seen.

He was seated with the others, just a small face in the crowd,
Not saying a word, or making a show, He never acted proud.
He didn't say to thousands, "You are eating because of me,
For I am the one who gave my lunch; you owe it all to me."

The little lad did, as we should, when we do for others,
An act that is good.
He quietly waited until he was served,
No mention is made that his voice was heard.

We are not even told that Jesus called his name,
Or called him out or gave him fame.
When we think of the miracle of the thousands fed,
The credit goes to Jesus, who blessed and broke the bread.

So, when we offer our gifts to the Lord;
We are not to expect recognition or seek rewards.
We give, as the lad, willingly and free,
Desiring only, to others, a blessing to be.

THE LIGHTHOUSE

Our lives should be a lighthouse, to those around us lost in sin,
We stand through all the sands of time, pointing the way to Him.
The lighthouse never moves, or changes in its place,
But continually shines the beams of God's redeeming Grace.

The light from the lighthouse shines
In directions all around,
But the lighthouse never moves,
From its foundation on the ground.

It stands upon the shore, so close to waves, and storms, and gales
But high above the waters, the light within the lighthouse,
Never flickers, never fails.

Many a man thought drowning, has caught the Gospel rope,
Thrown to him thru the message of Salvation, Light, and Hope.

The keeper of the lighthouse never leaves his post unmanned,
He stays on guard so faithfully, lighting the way for every man.

When all the ships of life's sea,
Have anchored to sail no more,
Many will gladly tell you, the lighthouse guided and led them,
To land safely on Heaven's shore.

Then, THE LIGHT of the lighthouse in Heaven,
Will bid us welcome ashore,
Where JESUS, THE LIGHT OF THE LIGHTHOUSE,
Shines in His Glory evermore.

LIFE'S PUZZLE

A giant puzzle is our life, made up of countless shapes,
When we first begin to solve it, we know not the form it takes.
Each day we find another piece has fallen into place,
And what we thought could never be,
Is accomplished by His Grace.

Sometimes the puzzle is hard to work, the picture hard to see
How any good thing could be found, from all life's mysteries.
The pattern of life's puzzle is hard to understand.
How so many different pictures, all come from God's own hand.

The pieces in life's puzzle are all varied in amount,
Some come together so quickly, it seems they hardly count.
While others toil thru many years, they sometimes face defeat,
There are so many trials and tears;
Before their puzzle is complete.

The master pattern for us all who trust our Saviour's Grace,
Is in the Book of Romans, found in chapter eight.
Where we find that all things that seem so out of place
Will come together for our good,
A picture of God's Grace.

THE LIFE IS IN THE SEED

I gathered the last of the garden;
The beds were empty and bare.
It had fed me well all Summer;
I even had veggies to share.

But the cold wind blew, and the garden was dead.
Not one thing was growing in the little raised beds.
Yet when Springtime came and I went outside,
The garden was green much to my surprise.

I thought, how can this be when it had been so clean?
But under the dirt, alone and unseen,
A little seed lay dormant
Hidden in the ground below,
Its nature inside was to wake and to grow.

Often, we think we are bearing no fruit;
No good things in life we seem to produce.
We feel we are useless and hidden from view,
No one seems to care or see what we do.

Yet just as the beautiful lily
Comes from the bulb deep in the ground,
We will rise in the Rapture
When the trumpet sounds.

The Goodness & Grace of God

And the Lord passed by before him, and proclaimed,
the Lord, the Lord God, merciful and gracious,
longsuffering, and abundant in goodness and truth,
Exodus 34:6

And of His fullness have we all received,
and grace for grace.
John 1:16

ABCS OF OUR GOD

Our God is AMAZING,
His BENEFITS never CEASE.
He DAILY comforts His children
And EMBRACES them with peace.

He is FAITHFUL to GUARD and to GUIDE us.
His HELP is there when we fear.
His INFINITE JOY sustains us,
For we KNOW He is always near.

His LOVE and His MERCY are present.
And NOTHING can hurt or harm.
When troubles or sickness surround us;
We can run to His OPEN arms.

He PROTECTS and QUIETS us
When problems seem to RISE.
He always has the answer;
Nothing takes Him by SURPRISE.

He TENDERLY watches His children.
He keeps them UNDER His wings.
His VICTORY and WONDERFUL presence,
Gives us EXTRA reason to sing.

So, YIELD your life and soul to Him,
With complete surrender and ZEAL,
And you will know these wonderful truths,
When you trust the God who is real.

GRACE
God's Riches At Christ's Expense

GRACE, can we ever imagine what is meant,
By God's Riches to us, at Christ's Expense?
What a price He paid to make Grace free,
And bestow it so freely, on you and me.

God could not look on the human race,
Corrupted with sin, and filled with disgrace,
His Holiness could not allow Him to look on sin,
That is where His marvelous Grace came in.

For Christ took on himself, our sins and ills,
And carried them all up Calvary's hill.
He was bound to the cross with nails of our woe,
No one but Jesus, could ever love so.

It was our transgressions He was wounded for,
It was our grief and sorrows, He willingly bore.
He was chastised to provide us with peace and good will.
It was by His stripes, we are made whole, and healed.

We were given God's Riches, at Christ's expense,
As up Calvary's mountain, He willingly went.
He gave all He had, his blood and his life,
This Free Grace we enjoy had a tremendous price.

GLORIOUS CHANGE

From the darkness of the cocoon,
To the glorious burst of light,
The butterfly emerges, to sunshine, out of night.

No longer bound as a caterpillar worm
But free and beautiful, the butterfly is born.
No longer hanging, covered and bound,
The lovely butterfly, a new life has found.

So, man, the lowly creature, even a worm,
Can be changed so completely and be reborn.
From the sinner so low, and doomed to die,
His soul can soar free, as the butterfly.

Change, glorious changed, how can it be
That God would set us lowly worms free?
No longer bound to earth's sin and despair,
We rise, as the butterfly, secure in His care.

Another change is yet to be;
When this mortal man finds immortality,
This cocoon of corruption that has man bound,
Will be shed, when we stand,
On Resurrection ground.

THIS SAME JESUS
Acts 1:11

This same Jesus the disciples saw go away
Is the same Jesus, who will return one day.
This Jesus who walked on the earthly ground,
Is the same Jesus we will see, when the trumpet sounds.

This Jesus who said, "Be holy as me."
Is the Jesus we will face in eternity.
When we stand at the Judgment and look on His face;
He'll say, "You are mine, I saved you by Grace."

When Jesus returns, He will be the same;
For He never changes, for God, is His name.
He cannot change, He is God evermore.
He that comes in the clouds, is He who walked on the shore.

When He walked on earth, He sinless remained;
He never allowed his soul to be stained.
He prayed that God would so keep His followers true,
He said, "May they follow me, as I follow You."

This same Jesus is coming for His Bride,
He expects to find spotless, with no sin to hide.
Her garments not wrinkled, nor stained with sin,
But adorned and ready, and waiting for Him.

This same Jesus who was spotless and whole
Is interceding for us and keeping our souls.
He prays that we are faithful and obedient will stay;
For soon He is coming to take us away.

THE CRUCIFIED ONE

Saved by the blood of the crucified One;
Jesus has saved me, the victory is won,
My sins are forgiven, my heart's white as snow,
We should tell this glad story, wherever we go.

Jesus was crucified to save you and me,
He gave His life's blood to set our souls free.
He died upon Calvary that we might have life,
He shed all His life's blood, to pay the great price.

He was buried in a tomb, but there He did not stay,
For God sent an angel to roll the stone away.
He left the tomb, with victory over the devil and Hell.
And we have been commissioned this story to tell.

He ascended back to heaven, sent the Holy Spirit to stay,
To lead men in all truths and guide them day by day.
The disciples tarried and prayed after Jesus went to Heaven,
Then with the sound of rushing wind, the Holy Spirit was given.

If you want your life to triumph over sin
Let the blood of the Crucified, cleanse you within.
Then surrender your life to God's Holy Will,
And your innermost being, the Spirit will fill.

THE WONDER WORKING POWER OF THE BLOOD

Without the Blood, the soul is lost,
It can never be saved, except thru the Cross
Eternal Life is in the Blood
That was shed by Jesus, because of His love.

The blood of Jesus always brings peace,
When it is applied the tears of sorrow will cease.
Peace cannot be bought with a price,
But was given to us, when Jesus gave His life.

When Satan tempts you with sin,
The blood applied, the victory will win.
The blood has power to cleanse, day by day,
The blood washes every sin away.

The blood of Jesus casts out fear,
It brings the presence of Jesus near,
Fear is cast out by perfect love,
Which Jesus was, when He shed His blood.

The blood can save no matter how low
The vilest sinner can bathe in its flow.
The blood of Jesus will cleanse from sin,
If we open our heart, and invite Jesus in.

THE PEARL OF GREAT PRICE

Some people think that Jesus is the Pearl,
Which we obtain, by giving up the world.
But we are the Pearl, which is of great price;
Jesus purchased us, with the blood of His life.

Man's life is lowly and has no worth.
He is nothing more than the dust of the earth.
He has nothing with which a pearl to buy.
He could not buy pearls, no matter how he tried.

The Pearl of Great Price, was wrought at the Cross
When Jesus suffered the tremendous cost.
A pearl is formed from suffering and pain,
It took the blood of Jesus, this pearl to gain.

Jesus gave up the splendor of Heaven
To hang on the cross, where His side was riven.
As water and blood came from His side,
The "Pearl" was formed, for which He died.

The true beauty of pearls is seen when they are strung;
Jesus purchased this pearl, on the cross, where He hung.
On cords of love, through the blood of the lamb.
God formed the Pearl of Great Price, from the sins of man.

God took the suffering and pain of His Son
And made the beautiful pearl to shine as the sun.
It's beyond comprehension that sinful man,
Is the Pearl of Great Price, in God's wonderful plan.

So, when you feel empty and worthless in life,
Remember, God calls you, the Pearl of Great Price.
His precious Son, Jesus, left Heaven above,
To redeem the Pearl of Great Price, with His sinless blood.

OUR BURDEN BEARER

If the yoke of the Lord is easy,
If the burden of the Lord is light,
Then why do we find it so hard
To walk in the path that is right?

It seems our burdens are heavy
Our yoke seems hard to bear.
We feel so heavily laden,
Surely there is no one who cares.

There must be something we are missing,
There must be a secret key.
We must not have learned what He meant;
When He said, "Come unto Me."

I think I have found the answer
I think the solution is there;
There's a condition to meet, when we lay at His feet;
Our burdens too heavy to bear.

He said in His Word, if we would listen,
When we bring to Him our petition;
We are to leave our burden, and pick up another,
For He told us to bear the cares of our brother.

So, we cry with despair, then who then will share
This burden so heavy for me?
Then we hear Him say, "Child, I 'll make a way,
You give your burden to Me.

So, if our Burden Bearer is Jesus
Then another's seems light to bear.
For He gives us the Grace, and puts a smile on our face,
When each other's burdens we bear.

THE ANGELS OF GOD

When God created the world and made woman and man;
He had another wonderful plan.
He said, "Man is weak and will need much care,
So, I will put my Angels around him, everywhere."

"When he sleeps, angels will guard his rest.
When he is tempted, they'll help him thru every test.
When he is in danger, they will stay close by;
He will never be out of their watchful eye."

When God had a message to send to man,
He sent his angels to tell of His plans.
When He was ready to send Jesus, His Son, to earth;
He sent Gabriel to Mary, with the news of His birth

When Lot was dwelling in Sodom's Plain
And God was getting ready, fire and brimstone to rain.
He sent two angels to rescue Lot and his wife;
Who bore them out, and spared Lot, his life.

When Sarah was ninety, and had decided that she,
Was never destined a mother to be.
The angels told Abraham of the son she would bear,
But Sarah only laughed, when the news he shared.

When Paul and Silas were bound in jail;
It was an angel who opened the doors of their cell.
When Peter, in prison, for deliverance prayed.
'Twas an angel who woke him, and sent him on his way.

When Jesus hung on the Cross where He was bound
Legions of angels were standing all around.
They were waiting for the words He would speak,
And they would take Him down, loose His hands and His feet.

As He lay in the tomb, He was not alone
For angels were with Him, waiting to move the stone.
They do at His bidding, and move as He wills.
His every desire, they wait to fulfill.

It is His angels He gives charge for our care,
When we need help, they are always there.
In any problem or distress that falls.
God sends His own angels, whenever we call.

His angels are too numerous to know
They wait for His bidding, and are willing to go,
To any child in trouble, or life's distress;
With present help of angels, He has promised to bless.

WHEN JESUS IS LORD AND MASTER

When Jesus is Lord and Master,
And we know He has full control,
When your trials come at His bidding,
His love and His peace, fill our souls.
The world can't understand our singing,
When our lives seem filled with loss;
For even in death and sorrow
We cling to the Christ of the cross.

When Jesus is Lord and Master,
When we give Him all that we claim,
Then no matter how deep the valley,
We know that our God still reigns.
He gives us a song in the darkness,
He keeps a smile on our face.
For He wants us to be His witness,
And let the world see His Grace.

So even when Death has invaded,
And even when sorrow has come,
We fear not the unseen tomorrow,
For we know He is leading us home.
He lights our pathway with gladness,
He fills our soul with His love.
He makes the crooked straight before us,
for He shelters our way from above.

He said He would never leave us,
He promised us strength for the day.
So, we will walk by His side gladly,
and sing as we go on our way.
So, no matter how Satan would hinder,
No matter what he puts in our way;
We will finish the journey we started,
And triumph in Heaven one day.

BEHOLD, YOUR GOD

The God who hung the moon and stars in space,
And put the shine on King Sol's face,
He made the waves of the mighty seas,
Yet He lovingly cares for you and me.

He made the mountains, and valleys grand
He declared the oceans, be bound by sand.
Yet, this Almighty God of all creation,
Holds us secure, in the palm of His hand.

He, who made the lightening flash and the thunder roar,
Wrote for the songbird, the musical score.
He, who put the fire in the lightning bolt,
Put the beautiful song in the Nightingale's throat.

Behold, this God, who created all
Yet tenderly waits to hear our call.
His arm is not shortened, nor His hearing dim;
He always helps, when we cry to Him.

John cried out, "Behold the Lamb,
Who takes away all the sins of man."
Beholding this God, we should all fall on our face;
And worship His Goodness,
His Mercy, His Grace.

OUR GOD OF ABUNDANCE

When God opens the windows of Heaven
Our earthly needs to supply,
He doesn't just give what we ask for but He graciously multiplies.

When we approach His Throne for help we need to be found.
He doesn't just "Grace" us,
But Grace, much more abundant, abounds.

When His followers were hungry and needed to be fed,
He multiplied greatly the fishes,
And a few small loaves of bread.

When the armies were wearied and the battle was long,
He opened the eyes of the soldiers,
And showed them the multiplied throng.

He said, if we would honor and obey His command,
Our days, would He not only lengthen,
But multiply us in the land.

When He comes back to earth to rule and to reign
There will be multiplied thousands with Him
To make up the Heavenly train.

For Revelation tells us, on white horses they will ride;
And white robed thousands times thousands,
Will be by the Saviour's side.

This great God of abundance cares faithfully for His own.
We have only to ask Him,
As we boldly approach His Throne.

He has all that we need in His bountiful store,
He willingly gives unto us,
Grace, and much more Grace, o'er and o'er.

GOD'S BEAUTY

October is the time of year,
That brings God's presence very near.
For when we see the beautiful leaves,
We know only a fool would not believe.

Such beauty would have to come from God's hand;
The colors are there, by His decree and command.
For He makes the trees, and all that we see.
What a wonderful world, for you and for me.

We visit the beaches and the mighty seas,
We visit the forest with the beautiful trees,
We fly in the planes through the clouds in the sky,
We take them for granted, and never ask, "Why?"

We hike in the mountains, and climb the hills,
We visit the valleys, where all is still.
We sit by the streams, where the waters flow free,
We never ask, "How these things can be?"

God's love is around us, in all that we see.
His beauty, His love, and His Grace, that is free.
If we accept His blessings, then we'll understand,
That all of this greatness comes from God's mighty hand.

GOD RULES

The things that never change with time,
Are the things made by God's design.
Who tells the Moon to rise at night,
Tells the Stars to shine, with their twinkling light?

Who tells the Robin where to build her nest,
Tells her in the Fall, to fly South, not West?
Who tells the Owl to sleep in the day,
And fly out at night, to catch his prey?

Who tells the Ocean to stop at the shore
Where a thin line of sand, lets it wash no more?
Who tells the Thunder to make its sound,
And the Lightening to flash, before the Rain pours down?

Who brings out the Sun with its golden rays,
To signal the start of a brand-new day?
All of Nature obeys God's command.
The only rebellion is in sinful man.

Man thinks he is in charge of his own life,
He thinks he acquires wealth, thru his work, and his might.
Man left to himself, will become a fool;
Until he acknowledges,
IT IS GOD, WHO RULES.

GOD IS IN CHARGE

The waves of the sea crash and roar
Yet come to a trickle, when they reach the shore,
They have to obey their Creator's command,
For He set the Sea's boundary, in a line of sand.

The winds may blow and the lightening flash,
The thunder sounds with a mighty blast.
But the storms will cease, and the winds will die,
All under the care of God's watchful eye.

A man may grow to be six feet tall,
And yet he thinks he is in charge of it all.
He thinks he is in charge by what he has learned,
But he finds he's no match for a tiny germ.

He thinks education has made him smart.
While forgetting Who controls the beat of his heart.
One little virus can change the whole world's system.
Yet man refuses, to bow, and to listen.

God is saying, "I still make the rules,
No matter what you were taught in your schools.
I have power to bless, and power to curse;
If you fail to obey, I can make it worse."

He is a God of Mercy, and He is a God of Love,
But He is still God who reigns in the Heavens above.
If we will listen, and obey His commands,
Our lives will be blessed in this wonderful land.

WHERE ARE YOU?

When God put Adam in the Garden of Eden
He came down to visit, every evening.
One day He came, and said, "Where are you,
Look at Me, Adam, what did you do?"

Adam knew he had disobeyed;
He knew the punishment would have to be paid.
He didn't want to look God in the face,
He thought he was safe in his hiding place.

Today, America, has fallen so far;
We think God cannot find us, where we are.
America thinks she can hide from the punishment due,
She doesn't want to answer God's question,
"Where are you?"

But God sees all, He doesn't have to ask,
We cannot hide, though we all wear masks.
He told us plainly, we can't hide our sin.
The Truth of God's Word will always win.

We think we can get by in our sinful ways,
We think there won't be a reckoning day.

Disease and catastrophes, earthquakes, and storms,
Thru all these means, God is trying to warn.
We all will answer God's final call.
We will learn at last, we're not smart, after all.

THE LOST LAMB

The Shepherd had tended the sheep all day,
And now, it was time to sleep, but he said,
"Before I retire, I will check again on my sheep."

So he went to the fold, and looked around,
But when he counted, there was one not found.
He said, "I know there was a hundred sheep of mine,
But I can only count ninety-nine."

He was tired and weary from working all day,
But he knew he couldn't let one go astray.
So, he sought for a light to help him see,
Said, "I can't lose this sheep, it belongs to me."
He retraced the places they had been that day.
He searched the meadow, where they had romped and played.
But he searched in vain, there was no sheep there.
He said, "Where can he be? I've looked everywhere."

He said, "I won't give up till he is safe in the fold,
I love this lamb more than silver and gold."
Just when he thought it was of no avail,
He heard a tiny cry, and a very faint wail.

Caught in the thicket of briars and thorns,
His little lamb was there, scared and forlorn.
Sitting high on his shoulders, the little lamb rode,
The Shepherd never thinking of the weight of his load.
But all the way home he rejoiced in song,
Forgiving the lamb for all he'd done wrong.

Our Great Shepherd, Jesus, God's Son
Will never give up on one of His Own.
When we wander off, and go astray,
He seeks us and calls us, to come back to His way.

GOD'S PROMISES

Every time we see a rainbow
We know God's promises are true,
For after every storm
The sun comes shining through.

Every time we plant a harvest,
We know reaping time will come,
And after every night of darkness
We see the rising of the sun.

After all the blasts of winter
The warm sun of summer glows,
For God's promises are faithful,
And He said it would be so.

While the Earth remaineth,
He declared Day and night would never cease,
He promised harvest follows seedtime,
And His promises, He keeps.

So, we should never doubt or worry
For God's promises are true.
We can cast our fears upon Him.
For He cares for me and you.

GIVE HIM PRAISE

The mountains and hills break out in song,
The trees of the field clap their hands,
The rocks cry out with a voice of praise,
All that is silent, is man.

All Creation is filled with praise,
They worship God, the Great King,
When we consider the works of His hand,
Why would we not want to sing?

His praise should continually be in our mouth
For His wonderful care for man.
He alone, is worthy of our adoration,
He alone provided,
Salvation's Plan.

MERCY

Sometimes we aren't aware it is raining,
It falls softly at night as we sleep.
The same is true of God's Mercy,
As He tenderly watches and keeps.

We could never exist without the rain drops,
Our world would be dying of thirst,
And so it is with God's Mercy,
He graciously sends to the earth.

Even the vilest of sinners
Partake of His Mercy, and Grace;
There would be no survival of mankind,
If for one moment, God turned His face.

Sometimes the rain falls so gently,
Refreshing, and reviving the land,
Sometimes a torrential flood breaks,
But all is controlled by God's hand.

The torrential rains of His Mercy,
Were poured out on Calvary's Cross.
As the blood gushed forth from His side,
Giving life to all who are lost.

Sometimes we receive Mercy
When we aren't even aware of our need.
We are spared many heartaches and sorrows,
For with tender Mercies, He leads.

His Mercies are new every morning
Sufficient for the day, the supply.
So, thank Him each day for His Goodness,
And His Mercy, on which we rely.

GIVE HIM PRAISE

Fourteen hundred forty minutes in every given day,
Can we not spare one of them, to bow our heads and pray?
One moment out of many, to offer praise and thanks,
To our Wonderful Heavenly Father, who has given us each day.

Jesus healed the ten lepers, and they ran away with glee,
But only one leper would return, to give thanks on bended knee.

If our children were as ungrateful, as we are to God above,
We would surely reprimand them, we want them to return love.
God sends His rain and blessing to the unjust and just, the same.
Even when they do not thank Him, and never call upon His name.

May we never be found guilty of withholding thanks and praise,
To our Father for the blessings, He sends each and every day.
We can praise Him for His pardon, and forgiveness of our sins.
We can praise Him for our healing, when we cry in pain to Him.

We can praise Him for deliverance, from the pit of our despair,
We can praise Him for His loving kindness and tender care.
When we have a need or problem, He answers every cry,
Everything we need, He is able to supply.

His ears are all attentive, He longs to hear our praise,
So, we should give more than a moment, to Honor Him with praise
Oh, that men would praise the Lord,
For His wonderful works to the children of men,
That is what the Psalmist David advised,
And we should all say, Amen.

THE SHEPHERD'S CARE

All sheep need a Shepherd, for they are prone to go astray,
They need someone to guide them and lead them in the way.
The Shepherd does not drive them, but quietly walks ahead.
The sheep know he cares for them, so they follow as they are led.

Sometimes a little lamb, has not yet learned to obey
And runs ahead, or stays behind, and finds he is in harm's way.
So, the Shepherd leaves the other sheep, to find the erring one.
He gently puts him on his shoulders and carries him back home.

Jesus, the Great Shepherd, knows His children are like sheep.
So, He calls and anoints Pastors, for their spiritual help, and keep.
If like the erring lamb, His children go astray,
The Pastor prays, and counsels them, to help them find their way.

Without a Spiritual leader, who has a Shepherd's heart,
The sheep will all be scattered, and the flock be torn apart.
Each day the Shepherd seeks and finds,
Where food and water are supplied.
The sheep all gladly follow, for on the Shepherd, they rely.

The Scripture tells us, all we like sheep have gone astray.
Jesus, the Great Shepherd, has shown to us the Way.
But on our earthly journey, we need someone to guide.
Someone to share our burdens,
In whom we trust, and can confide.

OUR HELP IS IN THE ROCK OF AGES

Life's Road is stony, and rough, and steep.
But the "Rock of Ages" our way will keep.
The rocks of life, are stones of Grace,
On which we climb, till we see His Face.

When the rocks of life, make us stumble and fall,
To the Blessed Rock of Ages, we quickly call.
He puts us up, upon the Rock of Grace,
Where we rest secure, in the light of His Face.

When the way is difficult, and hard to face,
Then He fills our path with sufficient Grace.
On the Rock of Salvation, He lets us stand.
Safe and secure, from life's sinking sand.

As the Psalmist of old, we can know first-hand,
How He lifts us up, and makes us to stand.
From Earth's miry pit, and crumbling clay,
He anchors us deep,
In The Rock, to stay.

IF I HAD BEEN THERE

If I had been in Bethlehem that day,
To see Baby Jesus, asleep on the hay,
I would not have known who was lying in the manger,
It would have seemed only, the birth of a travelling stranger.

If I had been in the Temple and seen,
The knowledge and wisdom, of one, not yet a teen,
I still would not have known, what I had observed,
It was just a child, well taught in the knowledge of words.

If I had been there when the lepers were healed,
Would I have known then, there was greatness revealed?
If I had been on the boat that day,
And saw One walking on water, coming our way.
Would I have realized this was not merely a man,
But ONE sent from God, who must have a plan?

If I had been in the Garden, and heard Jesus pray,
Then saw the Soldiers and Judas, come to take Him away,
It would be hard to believe what I had just seen,
And the miracle wrought, with the bloody ear scene.

If I had been at the Cross, and saw Jesus die,
Would I have known, it was for me,
"It is finished," He cried?
If I had been at the tomb on Resurrection Morn,
Would I have realized that New Life had been born?

I was not there in these times long ago,
But He left us His Word, so all men could know.
That life that began in that lowly manger,
Born among us, and lived as a stranger,
He became flesh, so He could die for us all,
Providing Salvation, from our sinful fall.

Though I was not there, I can truly believe,
That Salvation was purchased, for all to receive.

But there is a time and a place
That I can be there.
When Christ comes back to Earth,
And we meet in the air.

We may be alive when He comes for His own.
Or we may sleep in death, when the trumpet is blown.
But when the clouds roll away, and the Saviour appears.
This time, we can say,
"I am here! I am here!"

None of these times, I was there to observe,
But a great precious promise is found in His Word.
Those who are waiting for Christ to appear,
Will rise up, and meet Him,
AND WE WILL BE THERE.

HE IS OUR LIGHT

When the darkness of night has ended,
And the stars have faded away,
Still the Morning Star shines brightly,
To welcome us to the day.

When the day is finally over
Ere the curtains of night descend,
The Evening Star shines in the twilight,
Like a soldier, who is armed to defend.

It is though he is telling God's children,
The darkness is nothing to fear.
For as you see me before you,
So, the Keeper of your soul, is near.

The darkness He makes light before us,
The crooked paths will be made straight.
When the Day Star appears in His Glory,
When He comes thru the Eastern Gate.

He is the Star of the morning,
He is the Star of the night.
We are always to walk in His footsteps,
For He says, we are the children of Light.

Suffering & Trials

And he said unto me, My grace is sufficient for thee:
for my strength is made perfect in weakness.
Most gladly therefore will I rather glory in my infirmities,
that the power of Christ may rest upon me.
2 Corinthians 12:9

A WELL IN THE DESERT

If you find yourself in the Desert
And all around you is barren and dry.
When your provisions are all used up,
For water, and food, you will cry.

Looking ahead, all you see is the waste land,
The dry burning sand, and the sun.
All around you is death and destruction,
You think the end of your life, has come.

But wait, what is that in the distance,
Is it a Well of Water you see?
With lush green grass all around it,
And water, flowing, and free.

God never leaves one of His children,
In the desert to perish from thirst.
There will always be life giving water,
If we seek His Kingdom first.

There is a well in the desert that is waiting
When we reach the end of our way.
There are rivers of water that are flowing,
Giving strength for all of our days.

There are life giving streams in the desert,
And springs in the valleys and hills.
He says to all who are thirsty,
Take the "Water of Life" and be filled.

JOY WILL COME IN THE MORNING

Sometimes the night seems never ending,
We think the morning skies will never break,
It may be pain, or troubles pending,
We toss and turn, and stay awake.

But morning follows night
As in His Word, God decreed.
We find when dark has turned to dawn,
His Grace is there for all our needs.

No matter how dark the night
However long it seems,
Joy will rise with the sun,
And troubles will pass, as a dream.

Joy always comes in the morning
To chase the terrors of night away.
The problems that rob us of sleep,
Seem not so bad, in the day.

The golden rays of the Sun
Fill our hearts with hope and cheer.
Taking away the fears of the nighttime,
Driving away, our cares, and our tears.

Weeping will last for the night, says the Scripture.
But joy will rise with the Sun.
The troubles of night will be over,
When morning has finally come.

Joy will come in the morning,
And there will never again be night.
For Jesus, the Son of the Morning
Will be the Eternal Light.

THE WILDERNESS

When you find yourself in the Wilderness,
Where sooner, or later we all go,
God will lead you all the way through,
Teaching what He wants you to know.

Sometimes Joy is wrapped in Sorrow,
And Healing is wrought thru pain.
Success is achieved through Failure,
And Loss becomes real Gain.

Tears may last through the nighttime,
But Joy will rise with the sun.
Our Failures become great Lessons,
That is how Success is won.

When all our plans and accomplishments
Slip through our fingers, like sand;
Our efforts and works have all come to naught,
And the loss, we don't understand.

God's ways are far above our ways;
His thoughts, so much higher they are,
And when we see what He has in store,
We find is much better, by far.

As the Children of Israel learned long ago
In the Wilderness filled with doubt,
The Promise Land, was still in view,
And God faithfully led them out.

So, in this life, as we wander alone
Facing sorrow, and pain, and loss;
Success is ours when we let Him lead,
and go by the way of the Cross.

OUR HOPE IS IN THE CROSS

When we walk through what seems life darkest hour,
The Blood of the Cross still has all its power.
When sickness has come, and our health is gone,
The Cross makes it possible
To seek help at God's Throne.

When our hope is gone,
Our life filled with despair,
We can look at the Cross
And see how much God cares.

The Cross provided salvation's plan
Extending God's mercy, to fallen man.
So, look at the Cross, when you are brought low,
No one but Jesus, ever loved so.

His Love didn't end at the Cross,
If on the Cross, He remained
We would still be lost.

He rose and ascended,
And for us intercedes,
He sees all our hurts,
And has Grace for our needs.

GOD IS ABLE

There is something about a Christian,
He keeps his feelings inside.
His heart can break, and his spirit bow low,
But the smile on his face, is wide.

When the one he loves dearest is in distress
With sickness and pain so strong,
He holds his head high, and keeps looking above,
For he knows his God can never do wrong.

It's hard to be brave, when you feel so afraid,
And the future seems filled with dread,
But the God that we serve, will give you grace,
And pour the oil of gladness over your head.

We don't understand why sickness must come,
We try so hard to be true;
But remember, God always cares for His own,
And even in this,
He will bring you through.

WHEN DARK COMES AT NOON

What do we do when dark comes at noon,
When what we thought distant future, enters our life so soon?
When the things we thought were years away,
Arrive unexpected in the brightness of day?

We think that death comes in old age when our health is gone,
But it is darkness at noon time when death takes the young.
When a baby so small brings joy to our hearts,
All is sunshine and gladness, nothing looks dark.
But death's shadow covers the noon day sun,
And it is darkness at noon when God takes that child home.

When the young man is healthy and well, and strong;
His days are happy, his heart filled with song.
Then sickness befalls, and he becomes frail;
Then it is dark time at noon, as the sunlight is veiled.

So, what do we do, when dark comes at noon?
When our dreams are shattered, and the rose loses its bloom?
When life's unexpected hits us hard in the face,
What do we do, where do we find grace?

God made the darkness His dwelling place,
The shadows of darkness are His secret place.
So, when dark comes at noon, just look up in faith;
And your heart will be filled
With God's special Grace.

WHEN MORNING COMES

When the body is sick, and the spirit worn,
We wait through the night, for the dawning morn.
For no matter how long and dark the night,
We always feel better in the morning light.

When the brow is fevered, and we are so ill,
No relief is found in medicine and pills,
When hope seems lost, and life seems vain,
We seem to hear a glad refrain.

"In the morning, in the morning, joy we'll see,
When the morning light makes the darkness flee.
In the dawning of the morning sun,
We find all is better, for morning has come."

As we go through life and suffer woe,
And there's nowhere to turn, and nowhere to go;
We wait in the darkness and terrors of night,
Waiting for morning to cheer us with light.

It won't be long, until Jesus, the Light,
Comes forth in His Glory, and ends the night,
With the Resurrection shout, He will appear,
And sound forth the message,
Eternal morning is here.

OUR HELP COMES FROM ABOVE

Sometimes it seems we are suspended in time,
There's never a light, for the sun doesn't shine.
We are not able to tell when a new day begins,
For there is no difference in daytime, and darkness so dim.

It seems we are caught in a trap of the nighttime of gloom,
And the sunlight of day never enters our room.
It's a darkness so thick it can be felt,
Is this really where God has told us He dwelt?

When our countenance is never graced with a smile
For we see nothing ahead but long, lonely miles.
We never knew our hearts could hurt such,
And there's no one to give a kind human touch.

When we feel isolated, alone, and cast out
There's no calm of assurance, only more clouds of doubt.
When we think we've come to the end of our day,
If we listen, we'll hear Jesus say, "I am the Way."

When we feel no man cares for our soul,
When we feel rejected, dejected, and treated so cold.
When no human heart has compassion or love,
Our only help can come from Above.

But if we'll lift our tear dimmed eyes,
And turn our hearts toward the Heavenly skies,
Though no one on earth cares if we live or die,
We are never out God's watchful eye.

So, when our hearts are broken and crushed,
We can feel the Saviour's heavenly touch
We are the apple of His eye, His priceless pearl,
He will stay close beside us, through this unloving world.

OUR HOPE

When joy is turned to sorrow
And smiles are turned to tears,
The only hope that sustains us,
Is we know our Lord is still near.

He said He never would leave us,
He promises we are never alone.
When our hearts are too broken for healing,
Grace is still found at the Throne.

When expectations are turned to failures,
And dreams are turned to dust.
When light has turned into darkness,
It is then, we have to trust.

When our pathway in life is confusion,
When we don't know which way to go,
Then we hear the voice of our Saviour,
Saying, "Follow the way I will show."

No matter how deep the sorrow
No matter how many the tears.
The hope that will always sustain us,
Is the knowledge that Jesus is near.

THE SIGH

Sometimes a sigh is mournful
Sometimes it is relief.
Sometimes it is complete bewilderment,
Sometimes, it is disbelief.

A sigh is a way of expressing
Emotions we cannot speak.
When we are without explanation,
Even a sigh, is weak.

Sometimes our hearts are so broken,
Our spirit bowed under the weight.
Our inner man cries in desperation,
Then a sigh from within, escapes.

When life closes in upon us,
We think under the stress we will die.
We find relief, and renewal,
And our hearts heal
With a sigh.

SUNSHINE FOR SHADOWS

There's a truth about shadows we seldom see,
That the Sun must shine, or they cannot be.
A shadow is made when something interferes
Between us, and the sun, which is shining clear.

There has to be an object between us and the sun,
Or we could not see the shadow that is cast upon the ground.
You never see a shadow if you keep your eyes on Him;
But our lives seem full of shadows, when we're in the valley dim.

When we are on the mountain top where it seems, we touch the sky.
We never think of shadows, for our spirits are so high.
But when faced with sorrow, and to the valley go;
It is there we see the shadows, that alarm, and frighten so.

But a shadow has no substance,
It can never hurt nor harm;
And we would never be afraid,
If we kept leaning on His arm.

Even in the Valley of the Shadow of Death,
We have no fear, for we lean on His breast.
Earth's shadows flee away, when the sunshine appears,
So, we need not be afraid,
For The Son, is always near.

PEACE IN THE STORM

When the weather spotters chased the tornado,
They were caught up in the tornado's eye.
A frightening experience, to say the least,
They were sure they were going to die.

But they found in the tornado's center,
Was a feeling of peace, so serene.
So different from outward destruction,
It was not at all what it seemed.

The Christian song writer had learned this,
When he penned the words of his song;
"There is peace in the time of trouble,
And peace in the midst of the storm,
There is peace, though the world be raging,
In the shelter of God's arm."

So, when life's storms and tornados,
Are tossing around all we own,
We will find in the eye of destruction,
We can run to the Saviour's arms.

As the tornado's eye is peaceful,
Though the winds are raging, and wild,
When all we can see is destruction,
There is always peace for God's child.

He can speak, and the winds will obey Him,
He can order the storms to die.
He can speak to our hearts to trust Him,
For we are safe in His watchful eye.

YET

YET...in addition, another reason...
Up to now...nevertheless.

When life seems hard, and the road seems long,
When your heart is sad, and you have no song.
Just keep this thought, don't worry or fret.
You haven't walked the last mile YET.

When you want to give up, and say, what's the use,
It all looks bad, and that is not an excuse.
Just remember God's promise, He will never forget.
He's not through with you, just YET.

You say, the sun doesn't shine,
My dreams are gone,
And YET I think, I will just go on.
Brighter days will come, but not just YET.

"YET" is the future we cannot see.
What life holds for you and me.
For God has a plan, with no regrets,
It will all be revealed,
BUT NOT JUST YET.

ON WINGS OF EAGLES

When life's burdens increase, and we feel no relief,
And our hearts can no longer sing.
We turn to the Word, and His voice is heard,
"You can mount up as on eagle's wings."

On wings as the eagle, how can this be?
Can we really rise, and really be free?
As the eagle soars high above all, it seems he sings,
Even when there is no wind under his wings.

When the lightning flashes, and the thunder roars,
High above it all, the eagle soars.
The wind lifts him up, and higher he flies,
The earth far below to his piercing eyes.

Then the storm abates, and the wind is still,
But the eagle soars high, over valley and hill.
He locks his wings and soars with no end,
Even though under his wings, he feels no wind.

So, when we are tossed with winds and storms,
We rise high above it, on eagle's wings borne.
When our heart is broken, and we no longer sing,
No winds of joy we feel under our wings.

The eagle is the only bird that can soar with no wind,
On the strength of his wings, he knows to depend.
So, we need no source, other than our God above.
Who will carry us safely,
On His great wings of love.

WE WON'T ASK WHY

So many things in life
We cannot understand.
We wonder if the things we face,
Are really from God's Hand.

No answer to our problems,
And we often question, "Why?"
We say, someday, we will understand,
When we reach our Home on High.

We say, someday it will all be clear,
We'll ask when we are in Heaven.
We will find out then,
Why all these tests were given.

But this is so untrue,
It will never be.
There will be no questions on our mind
When Jesus' face we see.

We will find old things have passed away,
As we read in God's own Word.
For there, we'll be complete in Him.
No questions will be heard.

THE SUN STILL SHINES

Sometimes it seems the clouds hang low,
Our way is dark and filled with woe.
We think we cannot see a way,
To make it through another day.

But, if we could see above the clouds,
The sun is shining still.
Its golden rays will pierce the dark,
And our hearts with hope, will fill.

We know weeping may last for the night
But joy will rise with the sun.
The clouds will have to fade away,
In the rays of the golden sun.

There is never a cloud that can hang so low
That it will not flee from the sun.
So, our trials and troubles, will all pass away.
When the SON OF THE MORNING,
Has come.

WHEN GOD SEEMS TO DELAY

God told us in His Word
To come boldly before the Throne,
To find Grace to help in times of need
And make our petitions known.

We often kneel when we're distressed
And fervently seek His face,
When we need an answer to our problems in life,
And we need His favor and Grace.

When His answer is slow,
Or the answer is No;
We don't understand the delay.
We grow anxious and fret, and seem to forget,
That we must submit to His way.

His ways are above our mere mortal plans
He promised our needs to supply,
So, we must trust His Wisdom,
To give the answer that's best,
And on Him, to completely rely.

So, if God seems to delay,
Or hear not when you pray;
Just believe what He says is true.
All that we ask, and abundantly more;
He is willing, and able to do.

SEE HIM WHO SEES YOU

When Hagar was sent to the Desert
Abandoned, forsaken to die,
She felt so alone, but was soon to learn;
She was under God's watchful eye.

He saw her dire situation,
He knew there was no one to help,
So, He spoke so gently to her,
Through the Angel, He sent Himself.

She lifted her eyes to the angel,
And realized she could see,
The One who was watching over her,
She fell to her face, on her knees.

She said, "I have seen the One who sees me,
I know in Him, I can trust,
I will learn to follow His leading,
For I know His ways are just."

In our life when we feel forsaken,
We feel no one cares for our soul.
We can look in the face of our Saviour,
And know He is in full control.

He is ever watching over us,
He never leaves us to ourselves,
So, see the One who sees you,
Standing, waiting, willing to help.

ELIJAH, AND THE JUNIPER TREE

God came down to the Juniper tree,
It was the prophet, Elijah, He had come to see.
He said, "Elijah, remember the last time we met?
I was sending fire to burn wood you had wet.

"You were standing tall on Mount Carmel that day,
Only sixty-three words you had to pray.
You were proving Me to the prophets of Baal,
That I am Almighty, and I do not fail.

"So, what are you doing sleeping here,
Like one hiding from danger, and filled with fear?
I am the same God who sent fire from above,
Have you forgotten that I care, and I love?"

Elijah answered, "I am all alone,
They have killed all, and besides me, there is none.
I've nowhere to go, there are none to help,
And I could not face them all by myself."

God said, "Elijah, arise and awake,
Drink all of this water, and eat all of this cake;
You've a journey ahead of forty days length,
This nourishment will give you, much needed strength."

"But you are not alone, I have thousands more,
Who have not bowed to Baal, It is I who keeps score.
So, take of this food, arise to your feet,
You'll find as before, all your needs I will meet."

So, Elijah arose, took the drink and the cake,
And once again fought for Righteousness' sake.
He found, as we know, that God is always near,
If we be still, and listen, His voice to hear.

NOTHING

When my soul is empty, and barren and dry,
There seems nothing left, not even tears in my eyes.
I think all is vain, there is no use to try,
"You have nothing to give," my soul seems to cry.

But then, I remember the words that I read,
All is not empty, you have no need to dread.
Remember the cruse of oil that is here,
For the Oil is the Spirit,
Promised always to be near.

I will not leave you, you are not alone.
You are never with "nothing"
For you are My own.

When I am empty of self
And nothing possess;
The Oil is still here,
And His Righteousness.

WHEN THE BROOK DRIES UP

What will you do when the brook runs dry?
Where will you go, to whom will you cry?
What will you do when hope is dead,
And all you can see, is a dry brook bed?

What will you do when supplies run out?
When nothing's in sight, will you start to doubt?
What will you do, when you are filled with fear,
And you start to ask, "Did God send me here?"

When the Ravens don't show with the daily bread,
Will your heart become faint, and filled with dread?
What will you do when your throat is parched and dry?
What will you do? To whom will you cry?

Your next place may not be at Zarephath,
But God still knows, just where you are at.
So, if your find yourself by a dried-up brook,
Remember, God never had a child that He forsook.

LIFE'S ROPE

If you feel you are walking on shifting sand;
If it takes all your effort, just to stand,
If life looks dark, and you have no hope,
If you feel you've reached the end of your rope;

Just tie a knot and keep holding on,
On the other end, is a Mighty Strong Arm.
If you're afraid of falling and can't hang on,
God's got you in His loving arms.

He holds the rope that you cling to
He understands what you are going through.
So, when you reach the end of your rope,
The other end is secure,
Held by the God of all Hope.

WHEN WE WONDER, WHY?

It seems sometimes when we do our best,
To prove to God we can stand the test;
He gives us more than we are able to do
And we find it hard to believe His Word is true.

He says He won't give us more than we can stand.
He says He'll never turn loose of our trusting hand.
But when the way is dark, and the nights are drear;
We wonder is it possible, that He is still near?

When our hearts are broken, and our bodies are ill
Is it true that God could love us, still?
If He loves us so, why are we thus?
Is He trying to see if we still can trust?

He said there would be songs in the night,
He said our battles, He would be here to fight.
He said our paths would be made plain.
He said He would make earth's losses, our gain.

It's hard to trust when our health is gone
It's hard to walk, when the road is long.
It's hard to see through tear dimmed eyes
It's hard to accept, that His ways are wise.

But we know in our hearts that it is all true,
That He never stops loving and caring for me and you.
We know His way is best, though we don't understand;
We know enough to keep holding His hand.

We know, as Job, that our Redeemer lives.
We know there's a reason for the trials He gives.
We know there is a design, and a Master Plan,
So, for now, we'll keep holding to His nail scarred hand.

GOD'S ISLANDS

To be on an Island is to have water all around
For if there were no seas, no islands would be found.
The sea means separation, for it cuts the earth asunder,
And we think of islands mostly, in the phrase, "down under."

Sometimes we are on an island, when our souls are dry and bare,
But the water of His Word is around us everywhere.
We think of an island as a place of desolation,
And we sometimes feel marooned, and filled with desperation.

But an island can be a place of beauty that is rare,
Where we go to rest, and forget about our cares.
We think of island as a place of lush and green,
Where the bustle and hurry of life is never seen.

God promised in Isaiah He would make the crooked straight,
And sometimes upon an Island, is where He lets us wait.
While He plans our lives, and sets our goals,
He leaves us on an island, to refresh and cleanse our souls.

So, if you are on an Island, see it as a place
Where God has allowed you, to learn about His Grace.
Take advantage of the quietness, and let Him speak to you.
You will find your soul refreshed, and your spirit is renewed.

AFFLICTIONS ARE SHADOWS

When pain and affliction have come your way,
When you feel weighed down, and dark is your day.
When life seems hopeless and you are filled with fear;
Look up! It means Jesus is very near.

The affliction you feel is proof of His love
As He spreads His great wings of healing from above.
The shadow of His wings is the affliction you feel;
So, when you are afflicted, you know He is real.

When the shadows of darkness and affliction appear,
Look up, and rejoice, for we know He is near.
He bends low, and hides us in the shadow of His wings,
And casts out our fears, and makes our heart sing.

What is darkness to us, is God's secret place;
There we are covered with His love, and shadowed by Grace.
The shadow of the Almighty is His covering of love,
He comes to us gently, as on the wings of a dove.

When the winds of affliction blow like a cold winter blast,
He hovers oh so gently, and His wings, a shadow casts.
Then we know we're not alone, that the affliction we feel,
Is nothing but the shadow of the God we know is real.

WHY WE HAVE TRIALS

Would you like to know what God thinks of you?
Then consider the things He asks you to do.
He doesn't approach those too selfish to care,
When He has a mountain to climb, or a burden to bear.

When He needs a heart to burden for one,
Who is lost in the world, and doesn't know His Son,
He comes to the one that He can trust to care,
Who will take time to pray, and to share.

In the working world, when He has a place
Where someone needs to see the effect of His Grace,
He doesn't use buildings, or steeples that glow,
But He chooses one who is His, and will let His love show.

In the everyday life, and mostly at home
Is where the hardest trials are most likely to come;
Where we live with the ones who know us best,
And seem to delight in putting us to the test.

When God wanted a man to make the supreme sacrifice,
And offer his son, who was the light of his life,
He didn't go to Lot, who should have been the one,
To offer sacrifices for the wrongs he had done.

But He went to Abraham, who had tried to walk true,
So, remember that, when He comes to you.
You don't have trials because you've done wrong;
But He wants the world to see, you can keep a song.

He wants His Grace and Love to shine through you,
That's why you climb mountains, and valleys go through.
He wants to show the world what His Grace can do;
So be honored, and thank Him, if He calls on you.

I WISH I WAS A DOG

A young boy in a Juvenile Home was so unloved by his father,
he made this statement to the Chaplain.

When Dad comes in the room and his old hound dog is there,
He pats him on his ragged head and lets him share his chair.
He never kicks or scolds him but greets him with a grin.
Sometimes I watch from guarded place and wish, a dog, I'd been.

It seems he never speaks to me but greets me with a curse,
Sometimes he kicks or hits me, sometimes it is even worse.
But old hound dog lies by his chair,
With never a worry, or never a care.
He knows that Dad will treat him right,
He doesn't even put him out at night.

But if I do a simple wrong, he's filled with rage and hate,
I don't know why, I irk him so, you see, I'm only eight.
Sometimes, I wish I was a dog, and maybe Dad would care.
How great would be one day to hear,
"Come, Son, and share my chair."

It seems Dad doesn't understand, how he hurts and wounds me so,
Sometimes, I wish I wasn't here, but I have no place to go.
Maybe if I had been a dog my Dad would care for me,
For dogs are treated with more care, than he ever shows for me.

One day, I heard good news, that I was special too,
That Jesus died to save my soul, and God's love for me is true.
Sometimes, I wish I was a dog, so, Dad would care for me.
But it's good to know, I have a living soul.
For God, Himself, loves me.

Grief and Death

For if we believe that Jesus died and rose again,
even so them also which sleep in Jesus
will God bring with Him.
1 Thessalonians 4:14

NEVER ALONE

Sometimes we aren't present when our loved ones die.
We feel so cheated, for we didn't say goodbye.
We say, it is so sad, they died alone;
No one was with them to see the Death Angel come.

A child of God could never die alone,
A host of angels carry them home.
The angels were there, encamped all around
They were lifted so gently, without making a sound.

So don't despair, or worry, or fret,
That you were not there when your loved one left.
They were not alone, Heaven sent a band,
Of beautiful angels, to hold their hand.

God knew that you would not agree,
If He asked permission for them to leave.
So, while you weren't looking, He slipped them away,
Where they will suffer no more,
And you will join them one day.

THE CHRISTIAN'S CROSSING

She pillowed her head for a good night's rest,
But awakened to find she was on Jesus' breast,
For while she slept, an angel came,
And sweetly whispered and called her name.

He said, "You are tired, and you've faithful been,
Tonight, you have reached your journey's end.
You've come to the end of your days on earth,
But I've been waiting for you, since your new birth.

For you trusted Jesus, and you've lived so true,
And there's a mansion prepared and waiting for you.
You didn't have a lot of money, or what it could buy,
But wait till you see, what you have built on high.

I know your loved ones, and family dear
Will miss you so and wish you were near,
Your friends will miss your happy smile,
But they all will join you, in just a little while.

So, the Christian went with the Angel Band,
Where Jesus was waiting with outstretched hand,
To welcome her to her eternal home,
And she waits with Jesus till her loved ones come.

So don't weep for the Christian, for she is at Peace,
Her days of suffering and sickness have ceased.
Never again will she know despair,
And she waits for her loved ones,
In that land so fair.

JESUS KNOWS

Who knows how a mother feels
When her first born child lies cold and still?
Who knows how it hurts to say goodbye,
Who knows the anguish, too deep to cry?

Who knows how a loved one hurts
When his life's companion has left the earth?
Who knows the sadness a parting brings
When the heart feels it never again will sing?

Who knows how a mother or father grieves
When a child they have nurtured they have to leave?
Who knows the loneliness an orphan feels,
Who knows the heartache, even time cannot heal?
Who knows what pain a child must bear
When he has no mother for him to care?
When mother and father have said goodbye
Who knows how one feels, when they can't even cry?

Unless one has stood by a loved one's grave
And tried to be strong, to stand and be brave.
Unless one has watched a loved one go
To the Valley of Death, they cannot know.

But Jesus knows how a mother feels
Jesus knows the grief is real.
Jesus knows the loneliness and how the heart cries,
When to our loved ones, we have said our goodbyes.
Jesus alone, can be our comfort and friend.
He alone will be with us until the end.

So cast on Him, your pain and your grief.
Only in Him, can you find relief.
He alone knows how your heart bleeds,
He alone can fill your lonely heart's needs.

MOTHER IS ONLY AWAY

Today your heart is saddened
There is no joy or mirth;
For your mother you loved dearly has left this earth.
But don't despair or let grief fill your heart;
Because you won't always be apart.

Soon the clouds will roll away
And Jesus will appear.
Bringing with Him all the saints,
Including Mother, dear.
She has not gone, she is only away;
Waiting with Jesus for Resurrection Day.

Although your heart is heavy,
And you are left alone to mourn;
It is to this end,
All men are born.
Just rejoice in this disappointing hour,
That on her soul, the second death has no power.

Death is only the means of transporting souls
To their Heavenly Home and eternal raptures untold.
We have hope in Him, who is our life and breath;
And soon you will be with mother,
Where can never enter Death.

GRIEF

I saw a little bird in a tree by my house,
Sitting on a limb, as still as a mouse.
She wasn't chirping, or fluttering her wings,
It seemed she was sad, with no song to sing.

Then I looked on the ground beneath her feathered nest,
A baby bird lay dying, with blood on its chest.
Nearby was a cat, with blood on its paw,
The face of the mother bird,
Was the most pained I ever saw.

The heart of the mother bird was crushed with grief,
She flew to the ground, covered her young with a leaf,
Then back to the tree, I saw her fly;
It seemed she wanted to stay nearby.

For the bird on the ground was still her own,
With its life snuffed out, before it ever had flown.

We are like that little bird,
When our loved ones are taken,
But we have faith in our Father,
That even in Death, is not shaken.

Not a sparrow can fall,
That He does not see.
So, when death comes our way,
To His arms we can flee.

GRIEF

When our hearts are broken in sorrow and death,
And we lose the One we loved, more than our life's breath.
We can't understand why our loved ones are taken,
But still our faith in our Father, is not moved, or shaken.

But we say, "God, I don't understand
How could such sorrow come from your hand,
You are a God of love, so how can it be,
That You would take life's joy from me?"

We say, "God, this burden is too heavy for me,
Will I ever again, the sunlight, see?
How can I be sure this pain is from you;
I can never get over, but how can I go through?"

God said, "Grief is the price you pay for love,
For all the happy times that were sent from above.
Death has taken your loved one for a time so brief,
But the memories of love shared,
Will overshadow the grief."

HOME

The house where I live now
Is just a place to stay,
It is not where I feel welcomed,
When I come to the close of the day.

In days gone by, I loved our home
For you were always waiting there.
When nighttime came, and day was done,
Our lives and times, we shared.

A house is not a home
Without someone to share.
You don't look forward to the end of the day,
When your loved one is not there.

What made this house a home
Were the things that I now miss.
Your warm embrace, your smiling face,
And the kiss upon your lips.

But I console myself in knowing
That you have just gone before.
Your welcoming arms,
Your smiling face,
Now wait at Heaven's Door.

TO BE SET FREE

There is a plight that is worse than death,
To lose a loved one who still has breath.
To have a loved one with reason gone,
While the outward body lingers on.

It is like they vanish to another place,
They don't remember your name, or face.
You talk to them, and they don't understand,
They have already ventured to another land.

We will never know what it is they think.
They can stare you down, and their eyes won't blink.
They talk to you in a foreign speech,
It seems they slip beyond our reach.

Some days you think they know you well,
But in just a moment, it is like a spell.
A veil descends and takes them away,
This is not living, so for death, we pray.

We see our loved ones slip away,
With their mind befogged both night and day.
They seem to drift to a foreign land,
And we lose forever, the touch of their hand.

So, death is merciful, when it finally comes,
And takes these loved ones to their home.
To Heaven above, where they are well and whole.
Complete in Him, both body and soul.

WE WILL MISS MOTHER

When death comes so unexpectedly
It takes us unawares.
We are so grieved, and our hearts so torn,
We wonder, does God care?

For the heart of the home is the Mother
And the strength of a man, is his wife.
So how can we go on, when she is removed,
And taken out of our life?

We had so much more living to do,
So many dreams to realize,
Now they are gone, and we are left
With a heart that wonders, Why?

She was taken so quickly without a word,
No goodbyes, or tear-stained eyes.
The Angels came, and bore her away
To her Heavenly home in the skies.

We would never be ready to give her up,
To drink of this bitter and woeful cup.
For we loved her so, and want her here,
The Saviour called, and she said, "I am here."

We do not weep for Mother, for we know she is with her Lord.
We weep for her family, who will miss her so;
Our only comfort is in God's Word.

We know that God can only do right,
Though we don't understand why this had to be.
So, we will cling to His hand, until we are reunited
With Mother forever, in Eternity.

I AM NOT HERE, I AM NOW THERE

We are confident, I say, and willing rather to be absent from the body,
and to be present with the Lord.
2 Corinthians 5:8

Although I am gone from among your midst,
And am no longer here.
Just think of me as being away,
For I am in that land over there.

Remember the promise found in God's Word,
"Absent from the body, is present with the Lord."
To be in Heaven, is better you see.
I cannot return to you, but you can come to me.

I did not choose to leave, for life here is fine.
I enjoyed many years, God gave me a long time.
But where I am now, there will never be a night,
The Sun won't have to shine, for Jesus is the Light.

What lies before you here today,
Is only mortal flesh and clay.
A house in which I no longer dwell.
It is not "me", it is just a shell.

You cannot bury the real Me,
From things on Earth, I have been set free.
I've left behind all toil and strife,
And now, I have Eternal life.

So, dry your tear dimmed eves,
And look with eyes of faith,
Just think of me in Heaven,
And we will meet inside The Gates.

NOT ALONE

When you sit by the side of a loved one,
And their life is slipping away,
There is only a hole, where your heart should be,
And it hurts too much to pray.

The pain you feel, as you hold their hand,
And you know you can't make them stay,
You want their suffering to come to an end,
Yet you ask for just one more day.

So different from the time of the birth of a child,
When family and friends gather around,
To await the time to celebrate,
The cry of the newborn sound.

I think Heaven has a Waiting Room
And family, and friends are there.
They keep asking the question, over and over,
"Are they here?" "Are they here?"

So, when your loved one leaves your side,
They won't be going alone.
A band of Angels will carry them away,
Where Jesus, and loved ones,
Will welcome them Home.

I'll SEE YOU IN THE MORNING

I'll see you in the morning,
We often say to friends,
We mean it will be soon,
That we will meet again.

When we go to sleep at night
We say to loved ones near.
I'll see you in the morning,
For the Sun will soon appear.

We think it is only briefly
Till we chat as friend with friend.
We never stop to think,
We may never meet again.

I'll see you in the morning,
Is a grand and glorious thought
For we'll meet in God's Tomorrow,
When our earthly days are naught.

I'll see you in the morning
When the pains of night are gone,
I'll see you in the morning,
When the Victory has been won.

When this earthly toil is over
And time shall be no more.
I'll see you in the morning,
On God's Eternal Shore.

NOT AFRAID

And whosoever liveth and believeth In Me shall never die.
John 11:26a

"Not long to live" the doctor says,
Worried? No, not I.
For I know I have Eternal Life,
And I will never die.

In life, I've moved so many times
And lived in different places,
So, Death will be another change,
From Earth, to Heaven's Graces.

This mortal shell that holds my life,
May go through death's dark valley.
But o'er my soul, it holds no power,
It is just a vale of shadows.

I may dread the path that lies ahead,
It is filled with things unknown.
A home in Heaven, waits I know
When this mortal life has flown.

So, if I leave before you do,
Don't cry when I am gone.
Just trust in Him, who cares for me;
We will meet in my new home.

CHRISTMAS WITHOUT MOTHER

When we come home at Christmas and see your vacant chair
Our hearts will be so broken, because you are not here.
As we go from room to room, it seems we see your face,
And sitting at the table, someone else is in your place.

We tell each other not to cry, this Christmas seems so blue
We think we cannot face this day, without a hug from you.
But then we think we hear you say, now children, do not grieve.
Although I am so happy now, I did not choose to leave.

So, wipe those tears, and dry your eyes and look with hearts of faith.
It will not always be this way; you soon shall see my face.
I'm more alive than ever now; I am happy, well, and free.
Just keep on trusting Jesus, for you soon will be with me.

You always came to visit me, when it was Christmas Day,
It was my greatest pleasure, to see your children play.
But now I know what you enjoyed, for I am in your place.
I am with My Heavenly Father now, and safe in His embrace.

GOD'S COMFORTING ANGELS

I will not leave you comfortless, I will come to you.
John 14:18

When God sends the Angels for the still born child,
He says, "Bring them with much care.
Make your mission so gently, and swiftly,
The parents won't know you were there."

"For I will have to prepare them
For this fiery trial they face.
So, when you return with the baby,
I'll send the Angels of Mercy, and Grace."

"When they hold the lifeless form
Of this baby they loved so dear,
I will have the Angels, Comfort, and Peace,
To hover and stay so near."

"In the days ahead, when they are hurting,
They will find My Promise is true,
When I said, I won't leave you comfortless,
Not an Angel, but I Myself, will come to you."

The Hope of Heaven

For we know that if our earthly house of this tabernacle were dissolved, we have a building of God, an house not made with hands, eternal in the Heavens.
2 Corinthians 5:1

In My Father's house are many mansions:
if it were not so, I would have told you.
I go to prepare a place for you.
And if I go and prepare a place for you, I
will come again, and receive you unto Myself;
that where I am, there ye may be also.
John 14:2-3

ETERNAL LIFE

If You let us go to Heaven
For just a year or two,
It would make it more than worth it,
For a life of serving You.

Just to see the walls of splendor,
Just to walk the streets of gold,
Would make us glad, that we believed,
The Greatest Story ever told.

When we saw the Throne of Heaven
With the Saviour seated there.
It would fill our hearts with rapture,
Which nothing here can compare.

But You told us in Your Word,
That our life will never end.
That on and on, through countless ages,
In Heaven, we will spend.

Why You gave us life eternal,
Which we never could deserve;
Was because You loved us without measure,
Not because of how we served.

Through the eons, and the ages,
Where Time will be no more,
We will worship and adore You,
With Eternal Life forever more.

HEAVEN'S GATES OF PEARL

We often sing of the Pearly Gates,
That for the saints of God awaits,
We sing of the Gates we will enter in
When we are through with life's toiling.

The Gates are made of pearl, and not of stone,
A Pearl God made and wrought of His own.
Stones were created when the world began,
But the Pearl didn't exist, until man sinned.

Before the fall of Adam, no suffering was known
Everything was perfect, as the precious stone.
But when Adam fell, sin entered the race,
And suffering and toil, took perfection's place.

A pearl is the result of suffering and pain;
So, the Pearly Gate of Heaven, was gained.
As the anguish of the oyster produces the pearl,
So, the Gate of Heaven, is the sins of the world.

All our sins and afflictions on Jesus was placed
He bore them all without the Gate,
Through the hurt of the oyster, the pearl is formed,
In the sufferings of Jesus, our souls are reborn.

When God looked down from Heaven's Throne,
And saw Jesus covered with sins, not His own.
He had left all to redeem the Pearl of Great Price,
Sinners redeemed, by His blood and His life.

So, God took the sufferings and hurt and pain,
Back up to Heaven, where they would be gain.
The sufferings of Jesus, as He died for the world.
God took them and made Heaven's Gates of Pearl.

A PLACE IN THE PALACE

When you are tired of your self-filled life,
When you long for a heart that is new,
When you repent of your sins, and your selfish ways,
There is a place in the Palace for you.

A Palace is where Royalty dwells,
And only the family is there.
A stranger could never call it Home,
He has no right to share.

But if the King, adopts such a one,
And takes him to live as his own,
A stranger no more, but he finds by Grace,
In this Royal Palace, he now has a place.

There is a place in the Palace for you
When you accept Salvation,
And all things are new.

No longer a stranger, but adopted and loved,
There is a place for you,
In the Palace above.

HEAVEN, OUR YONDER HOME

"YON" is described as day after tomorrow,
Or a place far away, with no heartaches or sorrow.
A YON place is afar, but yet within view,
It is a much-desired land, which wise men pursue.

We speak of YON LAND, as much better than here
A land filled with sunshine, no hurt and no tears.
YON LAND is the future, where Time is no more.
For tomorrow never comes on Heaven's bright shore.

When Abraham was told to give his Son as sacrifice,
He said, "We will go YONDER, and offer up his life."
But YONDER on the mountain, was where they found God's Grace,
With the lamb caught in the thicket to take Isaac's place.

In the Garden of Gethsemane, Jesus told His disciples to stay;
He said, "I will go YONDER, and find a place to pray.
YONDER in the Garden, He yielded to God's Plan;
To drink Salvation's cup, for every fallen man.

YON LAND is our hope, where it is always bright.
For the lamb of God, Jesus, will be the only light.
For Time is no more, when Eternity dawns.
There is joy unspeakable, in that sweet LAND OF YON.

YON LAND is a special place
Where God bids His children come.
For HEAVEN IS THAT YON LAND,
It is our Eternal Home.

I REALLY GET TO GO

I heard about a Heaven where the angel's wings are white,
Where the sun is always shining, and there never is a night.
In childhood days, it was a dream, a place of beauty rare;
So wonderful and awesome, for Jesus Christ is there.

I heard it was a place, where the Gates are open wide,
For the Saved are made to enter, through Jesus's blood pierced side.
But it seemed a place of far away, a place of fantasy,
But when I trusted Jesus, I found it was FOR ME.

I heard that in this Heaven, there is no grief or woe,
But the greatest news I ever heard, I REALLY GET TO GO.
I heard there were no tears, no sorrows we will know,
But what amazes me the most, I REALLY GET TO GO.

I've never travelled much while on this earthly scene
I've never visited Royalty or knelt before earth's kings.
The truths about this Heaven are beyond our finite mind,
There are many things about it, on this earth, I'll never know.
But one thing I know for certain, I REALLY GET TO GO.

Yes, I'm really going to Heaven, you may doubt I know for sure,
But my sins have been forgiven, and my heart has been made pure.
And in His Word, He tells us, that the pure in heart He knows.
And He's prepared for me a Heaven.
AND I REALLY GET TO GO.

THINGS OF VALUE

We spend our time, our effort, our worth,
In acquiring things temporal, things of the earth.
We find in the end, these riches we seek
Are only borrowed to use, they are not ours to keep.

Eternal possessions can never be lost
If we accept Salvation, through the Blood of the Cross.
Treasures in Heaven, a home in the Sky.
The things that we own, are things we can't buy.

As we spend our days upon this Earth,
May we be ever mindful of what really has worth.
The riches of life, after which men seek,
Will vanish away, they are not ours to keep.

We should work for what we never can lose,
See these earthly possessions as only to use.
The Kingdom of God, and His Righteousness seek;
And Eternal treasures will be ours to keep.

Where men's treasures are, there will his heart be,
May we strive daily, this truth to see.
Not waste our days on what we will lose.
But live with Eternity's values in view.

We must keep our hearts focused on the Old Rugged Cross,
Count earthly possessions and riches, nothing but dross.
When our life is ended, if we have counted the cost,
We will be safe in Heaven, where nothing is lost.

LIFE'S JOURNEY

As we near the end of Life's Journey
It seems the road is all up hill.
When our strength is needed the most,
Our bodies are weak and ill.

With a backward look, we can see how far
This winding road, so rough and steep,
Has brought us to where we are.

The road was long and tiresome,
With pitfalls along the way,
But we stayed the course, and with God's help,
We can see the close of the day.

The memories we have of a life that is sweet
And we cherished each happy day.
But also, we had many heartaches and tears,
As we travelled life's winding way.

The road ahead looks brighter still
And we climb with no fear or dread.
We know our Father waits
To welcome us Home,
And the best is yet ahead.

LIFE'S PATHWAY

As I travelled down life's pathway
My heart was filled with dread.
When I saw how tedious and treacherous
Was the road that lay ahead.

The road was twisted and winding
Dangers were hidden from view.
And I feared my footsteps would falter,
And I could not make it through.

There were pitfalls and side roads,
And obstacles I could not climb.
But I edged my footsteps onward,
Putting the fears from my mind.

The road was ever so curvy
And I could not see an end.
My heart was faint within me,
Dreading the unknown bends.

Then I looked over my shoulder
To see the progress I had made.
But the road I had travelled, had disappeared,
I saw only green pastures, of shade.

Then I remembered what His Word had said,
That the crooked paths, would be made straight.
And beside still waters, He would lead
To the end of life's road
Where Heaven awaits.

AS THE LEAVES OF A TREE

In Wintertime, when the trees are bare
They look so cold, with no leaves to wear.
They stand stripped of the foliage that graced them so,
Chilled and shaking, when the North wind blows.

Just a few days ago we enjoyed the shade
Their leafy boughs provided on the hottest days.
Now they lift their limbs outward, as if in prayer.
Their coats of lush green, they no longer wear.

The silhouette they make just before dark
Looks stately and proud, though barren and stark.
They stand like Kings, still wearing their crown,
There's no weight on their branches to bow them down.

The trees are like mankind, in time of old age,
He finds the pleasures of life, as leaves, pass away.
Life's possessions and riches, that he treasured so,
Now slip from his grasp, as leaves, when winds blow.

He stands as the trees, stripped and bare,
For the things of this life, he no longer cares.
From things temporal and earthly, he soon will be free.
His life will vanish, as leaves from a tree.

Each Springtime the trees are a beautiful scene.
As each one is clothed with a new coat of green.
So mortal man will find in the Resurrection Day;
Clothing of immortality has replaced mortal clay.

AS A BRIDE ADORNED

A bride adorned, what a beautiful sight,
As she walks down the aisle,
In a gown spotless white.
She has been preparing for quite a while,
Before we see her coming down the aisle.

Her gown has no wrinkles, her hair must be groomed,
She strives for perfection,
When she enters the room.
As the Bride of Christ, we have much work to do,
From the veil on our heads,
To our dress, and our shoes.

The veil of our mind, must be clean in thought,
The gown of our works,
With His Blood, He has bought.
Our feet shod with the Gospel,
We are commanded to wear,
As the news of Salvation, we continually share.

So, when we, as a Bride, take our place by His side,
From the Father Himself,
There will be nothing to hide.
As He says to His Father, "I present My Bride."
May we be so prepared,
He can say it with pride.

PLAIN AIR RIDE

I've never been in a plane,
Never been off the ground,
But that's gonna change one day,
When I hear the trumpet sound.

I won't need a ticket,
Or an assigned seat,
We'll all go together,
When in the Clouds we meet.

We won't need a pass
To get on board,
Just the words, "Come up hither,"
From Jesus our Lord.

There's no luggage to check,
Or lines to go through,
Just answer the call
From the skies so blue.

We will pay no fare,
Though high was the cost,
The Blood of God's Son
Paid for all who are lost.

You are welcome to join us
For this Plain Air Ride,
For it was for you
That Jesus died.

IF

If the souls you win, and the deeds you do
Decide your fate, when your life is through...
If the ones you help, and the time you give;
Decide in Eternity, where you will live...

If what you give, and the time you share,
Decide in Glory, what crowns you wear...
If the ones you've helped, and the souls you've reached,
The example you've set, that your life has preached...

If this is the measure of the rewards you win,
When before the Judgment, you finally stand...
If the miles you've travelled, and the sacrifices made
Account for your standing, to receive your grade...

If all of these "ifs" are true, and they are,
This will be your reward at the Judgment Bar.
We know that by works we don't enter in;
But by trusting Jesus, for forgiveness of sin.

We work to win trophies to lay at His feet
When before Him we stand at the Judgment Seat.
If you have been faithful, and many souls won.
In that Great Day, He will say, "Well done."

THE ONE-WAY STREET OF LIFE

Our journey through life is a one-way street,
It leads to a destiny we all have to meet.
There are no detours, or side roads,
No U-turns allowed.
We move ever onward with the maddening crowd.

Some move forward at a steady pace,
Others stumble and fall, with an unsteady gait.
No one comes towards us, all face the same way,
There is no turning back,
On this Road marked, "One-Way".

There are curves in the road and hills to climb,
Sometimes it is dark, sometimes the sun shines.
Our fellow travelers often lighten our load,
Sometimes we're alone, it's a long, lonely Road.

There is no turning back on this One-Way Street.
We move ever onward, our destiny to meet.
Life's journey is not only a street of One Way,
It is also a Toll Road, with prices to pay.

Sometimes the fee seems more than what's fair,
And a travelling friend offers to share.
The farther we go, the quicker the pace,
And we realize soon, we will end this race.

We keep going, but we have no fear,
We know not when our Exit will appear.

"NO RETURN TO LIFE'S ROAD" the exit sign reads,
There is no choice given,
It is a sign we must heed.

But when we exit Life's Road
And arrive at the end.
The next sign will read,
'WELCOME HOME, ENTER IN."

Our journey began when we accepted God's Son,
Who paid the great price to bring us home.
Though the journey was long,
And we oft failed to obey,
He never left us, to find our own way.

So, this One-Way Street
Is the way called "Straight"
Leading us Homeward
To where Heaven awaits.

AT THE JUDGMENT BAR

When you stand before the Judgment Bar
What will the great books hold?
Will you be turned to outer darkness
Or dwell in the City of Gold?

All your records will be there to face,
For the eyes of the Lord are in every place.
You will give an account of all that you do,
What will the books tell of me and you?

If your name is in the Book of Life
Then all for you will be well.
But if there your name is not found,
You will be bound and cast into Hell.

All are made equal at the Judgment Seat
There'll be no poor, there'll be no elite.
There will only be two classes, and He
Will say, "Enter in" or "Depart from Me."

If you work iniquity, you will have to depart,
For none shall see God, but the pure in heart.
Which will it be on the Judgment Day?
Now is the time to decide,
So don't delay.

WE WILL RISE

Long ago when the world began,
God came to earth to commune with man.
He first came to Adam, and Adam knew,
He had done what he was told not to do.

Adam and Eve saw a very sad day,
When for disobedience they had to pay.
This beautiful home where their life had begun,
They had to leave, and never return.

Then God came down and took a walk;
With a man named Enoch, God had a talk.
He said, "You've been faithful, and followed me,
So, from the jaws of death, I am setting you free."

God took Enoch home with Him that day;
Left his friends wondering why he went away.
They never found Enoch, and never knew why,
But Enoch was safe, in his home in the sky.

Many years later, Elijah's story was the same.
In a fiery chariot, he left in a flame.
Carried to Heaven, without having to die,
Elisha watched him disappear in the sky.

We may be caught up like Elijah,
When the trumpet sounds,
Or at rest in the grave and rise from the ground.
When He comes for His own, we will rise in the air –
To be forever with Jesus, His glory to share.

RESURRECTION

You can be buried in a suit of silk,
Or buried in a body bag;
It won't matter when Jesus comes,
It will be cast off as a rag.

You can die at sea, or burn in a fire,
But when Jesus comes, you will go up higher.
You will say, "O Grave, you can't hold me,
And Death, you have no stinger, you just buzz like a bee."

When death takes our loved one, we surely will grieve,
But it's just a short time to those who believe.
We will soon be reunited in Heaven to stay,
It will all be made right, on Resurrection Day.

Although you will cry, and your heart will be torn,
Just remember soon, comes Resurrection morn.
The skies will open when Jesus appears,
No more death, nor sorrow, no pain, no fear.

So, look up, dear Christian, it won't be long,
Till Christ returns, and we all go home.
Just trust His Grace, believe His Word;
We soon will rise as the wings of a bird.

The Beauty Of Creation

For by Him were all things created, that are in Heaven,
and that are in earth, visible and invisible,
whether they be thrones, or dominions, or principalities, or powers:
all things were created by Him, and for Him:
and He is before all things, and by Him all things consist.
Colossians 1:16-17

THE WIND

Sometimes the wind is just a rustle in the leaves,
Sometimes it is as soft, as a gentle ocean breeze.
Sometimes it is fierce, as the strong winds blow,
Creating blizzards from the falling snow.

Sometimes the trees are bowed to the ground
And the limbs break off with a thundering sound.
While the wind is always hidden from view,
We are well aware when it passes through.

When the days are filled with oppressive heat,
Just a small breeze is such sweet relief.
The same gentle breeze, that is pleasant and warm
Can become a tornado, or a terrible storm.

God's Spirit, like the wind is always here,
Sometimes it is quiet, as a whisper in the ear.
Other times it is forceful as the rolling thunder,
And we stand in awe of
God's Might, and His Wonder.

THE LITTLE STAR

The little twinkling star hid behind a cloud,
Said these words, as he thought out loud.
When morning comes, and the stars fade away,
I'm going to see how it feels,
To shine in the Day.

I'm not leaving when the others fade away,
I want to see how it looks in the day.
The cloud answered the little star,
With words from on High.
You can't stay here, no matter how you try.

In God's Master Plan and Design,
He made the night for you to shine,
The Sun rules the Day, and the Moon, the night,
And you help the Moon with your twinkling light.

The little star said, "No, I am going to stay,
I want to see how it looks in the Day.
If you float away and leave me behind.
I'm going to show you,
In Daylight, I will shine."

But when morning came, the little star,
Couldn't see the Sun,
It was too far.
So, he submitted to the Creator's design.
And when nighttime fell,
He was happy to shine.

THE NIGHTINGALE'S VIGIL

The nightingale on my windowsill, stayed through the night,
But his voice was still. I said, "Little bird, what is so wrong,
That you have lost your comforting song?"

He said, "Oh, no, I have my song. It is right in my heart
Where it's been all along.
But see these ruffled feathers on my throat,
Where I have been injured, and stifled the notes?

"So now for the present, I have to be quiet, but I'll stay here
To comfort you, all thru the night.
You see, God permitted my voice to rest,
While my body heals, I must go thru this test.

"It's hard not to lift my voice in song,
Especially when the nights are so long.
But inside I'm still singing, my heart is still light,
And soon once again, I'll share my songs in the night.

"While I'm waiting so patiently, for my body to heal,
Inside of my heart, God's peace is so real.
When this trial is over, and I'm permitted to sing,
I'll lift my voice, in praise to His Name."

I said, "Little bird, we miss your lovely song,
While you are silent, in this trial so long,
When the time of your healing is finally o'er,
Your songs will be sweeter, than ever before."

THE FALLEN LEAVES

I watched the leaves as the Fall winds blew.
They were all turned brown, for Summer was through.
No longer needed to provide shade from the Sun,
The purpose they served, was over and done.

In the breeze they trembled, and shook, and twirled,
And one by one, to the ground they were hurled.
They tried to cling and fought to hang on.
But the Wind was stronger, and always won.

We are like those leaves, as to life we cling,
We don't like to turn loose of our self-made dreams.
The winds of change, we try to refuse,
But like the leaves of the tree, we always lose.

Our life is fleeting like the trees and the grass,
Our time on earth, too quickly will pass.
No matter how strong our grip on this earth,
Our days have been numbered from the time of our birth.

But we are different from the leaves that fall.
They just blow away, and don't matter at all.
When our time Is over and we break earthly ties,
We find we're Eternal, with souls that don't die.

If we have been like the tree that bears good fruit,
If we have been faithful and built on God's Truth,
Though our bodies, like leaves, will return to the dust,
We'll be safe in Heaven, with the Saviour we trust.

THE SNOW

Today I awakened and stood at my windowsill.
The whole world before me was silent and still.
Nothing moved on the earth, or made a sound;
For a blanket of white covered the ground.

It isn't necessary for the thunder to roll
For man to see, that God is in control.
He can send something so soft and light,
That man cannot stop with all his might.

Man cannot stop the snow from coming down;
It falls while he sleeps, without making a sound.
It is so gentle, so soft, and light;
And man is helpless in this blanket of white.

Sometimes God allows man to see
How totally helpless he can be.
With the snow that comes from God's mighty hand
He alters all of our best laid plans.

The mighty jets and trains that go
Sit quiet and motionless in the snow.
We have rockets and planes that travel in space,
But they sit, earthbound, by the tiny snowflakes.

When God looks down on this winter scene
He sees His creation, white and clean.
For the snow that has fallen, covers the dirt,
And God sees a peaceful and beautiful earth.

He is reminded of His promise, made long ago;
To wash our sins, whiter than snow.
As the world is made white covered with snow;
So, our hearts are made pure by Calvary's flow.

WE CAN LEARN FROM THE GEESE

When the geese go South for the winter,
They fly in the form of a "vee".
They fly so high in the great blue sky;
They are a wondrous sight to see.
They are a noisy bunch as they fly along
They create quite a stir in the sky.
As you watch them go, you may wonder why,
They are so loud as they fly.

They stay in their place as they fly along;
They never leave one behind.
But the form of a "Vee" is there to see,
For they fly in accord with one mind.
Their leader out front has no one to help,
As he takes the brunt of the wind.
But the geese that follow, all help each other
As they flap their wings in the wind.

They know the leading goose is on his own
So, they encourage him with their kind of song.
So, the honking you hear, is really a cheer
Saying, we're right behind you, don't fear.
They know he faces the strongest wind,
He is the first to fly into the storm;
So, they cheer him on, with their honking song,
And thank him for being their friend.

We like the geese, have a leader out front
Who is not afraid to face the storm's brunt.
Who will keep us going when the winds assail;
And help us through life's stormy gales.
We have such a leader in Jesus, our Lord,
Who picks us up, on the wings of His Word.
He will never leave us to fly on our own.
So, we should praise Him in song.

THE FIRMAMENT'S SHOW

On a Summer night, when the rain is through,
A beautiful Moon comes into view.
An unseen Hand parts the curtains of clouds,
And we see the Moon, so magnificently proud.

He appears in the Sky, with a golden glow,
Welcoming Earth, to the "firmament's show."
He says, "I will shine my brightest for you,
And millions of Stars you will also view."

He says, "Our Creator and Director has made us to shine,
We are all performing by His Master Design.
Each night you're invited this display to see,
There is never a charge, all performances are free.

"All that we ask, as this show you view,
Is that you give honor and credit to whom it is due.
When you return to your home, and go in for the night,
Give thanks unto God, for these glorious lights.

"Before I go, let me say this,
The coming attraction, you don't want to miss.
When we fade away, and the new day is begun;
You will be greeted,
By the Magnificent Sun."

THE NIGHTINGALE'S SONG

The nightingale's song is the sweetest of all;
No other bird has such a lovely call.
All the birds sing, and warble their praise,
They sing loud and clear, all through the day.

But the nightingale waits and saves her song;
Till the sunshine has ended, and the night is so long.
In the darkness of night when the shadows lengthen,
Then the nightingale sings, and her voice is strengthened.

It seems the darkness brings out her song,
Her notes trill more clearly when things have gone wrong.
When all else is silent, and time seems to stand still;
God sends the nightingale to our windowsill.

Sometimes, when our bodies are wracked with pain,
The nightingale comes and sings her refrain,
God said He would let the birds sing in the night,
To give His assurance that all is still right.

When our health seems to fail, and we are filled with fear,
We begin to wonder, does God care? Does He hear?
So, when night times of pain, and sickness grow long,
Listen closely, and hear, the nightingale's song.

THE CLOUDS

Sometimes the clouds are snowy white,
They move through the sky, like birds in flight.
Other times they hang low, and are heavy and grey,
They seem not to move, as they darken the day.

Sometimes they are scattered in patches of blue,
Sometimes the whole sky, is a dark ugly hue.
Sometimes they are outlined in edges of gold,
Sometimes they are filled with rain, sleet, and snow.

The clouds ever change in shape and in size.
Sometimes not a one is seen in the sky.
For the rising Sun drives them away,
Producing a beautiful, unclouded day.

We think of the clouds in a negative way,
We think what is perfect, is a Sun filled day.
But the clouds are needed for life to sustain,
They bring protection from heat,
and the wonderful rain.

So, when the day is cloudy,
Or the Sun is shining bright,
Just give thanks to your Heavenly Father,
For He knows just what we need,
And what He sends, is right.

THE RAINBOW

If we could see the Rainbow,
While the storms were raging on,
We wouldn't be so fearful,
And our faith would stay so strong.

But when the storms of life surround us,
And the winds of grief assail,
Our hearts are made to tremble,
And all hope, begins to fail.

While the skies are dark and stormy,
And the thunder crashes roar,
The lightning flashes fiercely,
And the rains begin to pour.

We long so for the sunshine,
And for the storms to cease,
But when our eyes turn upward,
Our hearts are filled with peace.

For we know who watches o'er us
And our lives are in His care.
And when the storms are over,
The Rainbow, that He promised,
We find, is always there.

THE HOPE OF SPRING

The Winter season is long and dreary,
We get so downcast, so tired, and weary.
The days are so short, and the nights so long,
And many days go by without a song.

But one day we look out, and what do we see?
The crocus is blooming, and the Robin is in the tree.
Our hearts spring to life with hope,
And our spirits are made strong,
We are so encouraged by the Robin's song.

God said as long as there is an earth,
There would be Springtime, and Nature's rebirth.
He said seed time and harvest would never cease.
That the rains would give the land's increase.

His promise is true. He has never failed yet,
And you can be sure, He will never forget.
He knows each little Robin, that says Spring is near.
So, surely, He knows you and all of your fear.

So, if your burdens are heavy to bear,
The God of All Comfort is standing so near.
As surely as Spring follows Winter's cold.
So, He sees you, to sustain, and uphold.

SPRING

I saw the birds fly swiftly by,
I heard the Robins sing.
I saw them all, and heard their cry,
Winter is past, it is now Spring.

The Winter was long, the days were cold,
But now 'tis Spring, called the Robin, so bold.
The days grow longer, the breeze is gentle.
For it is God's plan, that Spring follows Winter.

The trees start budding, the flowers appear.
Men and boys get out their fishing gear.
Spring is a time for love and romance.
Spring is planned by God, and not just by chance.

Spring is a time of new life and rebirth,
For the grass that died, reappears on the earth.
It is a time of beginning again for man.
We see God's love, in the Spring He has planned.

FLOWERS

Flowers are like God's Promises
There is one for every care.
If you take the time to look for them,
You will find they are always there.

Some grow high in the mountains,
Some in the valleys low;
But flowers, like God's Promises
Are there, when we need them so.

So, cherish every promise,
Found in God's Word so true.
And they will brighten every moment,
Just as the flowers do.

THE BUTTERFLY

The butterfly's visit is always brief,
For a fleeting moment, it lights on a leaf.
Like a Heavenly messenger whose only duty,
Is to bless our lives, with wondrous beauty.

So, if a butterfly you see on your way,
Know that God, is visiting you today.
In this tiny creature, with beauty so rare.
God is showing His Mercy, His Love, and His care.

LIVING WATER

How refreshing and cool
Is the mountain stream,
With the air so crisp,
And the trees so green.

When we are weary
And filled with care,
Nothing revives,
Like the mountain air.

When our souls are thirsty and dry,
In John chapter seven,
We hear Jesus cry,

"If any man will come,
Living Water, I will give,
He will never thirst again,
And Forever, He will live."

THE SPARROW

Psalms says God provides a house
For the sparrow to dwell,
And without His knowledge,
Not one ever fell.

The worth of a sparrow is not even a cent,
Only three fourths of a penny,
For one is spent.

If God takes notice of something so small,
Surely, He cares for us, when we call.
Our worth is far more than a bird in the sky,
Because for our souls, He sent His Son to die.

So don't be discouraged and feel cast out,
God's Word is true, you don't have to doubt.
If He cares for the sparrow, whose life is so brief.
He is surely concerned with our cares, and our grief.

The Almighty God, who gave the birds wings to fly
Is always attentive to our every cry.
So, when you are sad, and feeling depressed,
Just trust in His Love,
And lean on His breast.

THE ROSE

The Rose, so beautiful, delicate and fair,
With its radiant fragrance,
None can compare.

In describing Christ, The Psalmist chose,
To compare His beauty To Sharon's rose.
Lily of the Valley, and Sharon's sweet rose,
Speak of Christ Jesus,
Heaven's Sweet Rose.

The love portrayed by the rose so red,
Speaks of the Saviour on the Cross as He bled.
God's Rose was crushed,
And the fragrance released,
Was
SALVATION
MERCY
LOVE
AND
PEACE.

LOOK UP

When you feel alone in the evening
And darkness falls on your way.
The golden sun, as it is setting;
Sends forth its beautiful rays.

There is never a cloud that can linger
When the rays of the sun break through.
Sending a message of love from Heaven,
In letters of gold, to you.

You can lift your eyes to the Heavens,
And what a wonderful sight to behold,
The clouds that seem so threatening
Have become a canopy of gold.

MOONLIGHT

As the moon appears in the twilight
And the stars shine from their place;
The beautiful glow of the moonlight
Makes us aware of God's Grace.

The moon is only reflecting
The light received from the sun
And as evening fades into darkness,
The toils of the day are done.

As God lights our way in the daytime
And our hearts are happy and light,
The moon beams shine to assure us,
God is in His world,
And all is right.

SUNSET

Sometimes we welcome a sunset
For we long for rest and sleep,
And as darkness invades the evening,
We are filled with a sense of peace.

In old age, the time of sunset
Sometimes brings anxious fears,
But we know our Heavenly Father,
Has promised to always be near.

So, enjoy the beautiful sunset
As it signals the close of the day,
We can rest in the peaceful evening,
Knowing God keeps our way.

THE LILY

Consider the lily; it neither toils, nor spins,
Yet in any beauty contest, the lily will always win.
Consider the lily, such beauty and grace,
Does nothing itself, to achieve this lofty place.

From the bulb buried deep in the ground below.
Comes the beautiful lily, pure and white as the snow.
We see God's love in the lily so fair,
As we trust our lives to His omnipotent care.

LIFE

The Fall of the year is a lonesome time,
As the flowers and leaves all die.
The crisp Autumn winds have a mournful sound;
It is as if Nature sighs.

The warm Summer sun, and the warm Spring rains
Are replaced with sleet and snow,
And the days grow short, and the nights grow long,
While the cold North wind starts to blow.

Our lives, like the Seasons change each day,
And Wintertime comes so fast.
Our youthful Springtime, and Summer days,
Too soon, are over and past.

It seems, we just begin to live
And savor and enjoy each day;
When all too soon, these mortal shells,
Begin to fade away.

Our youthful steps, our energy keen
And strength to do as we will;
We find each day, is slipping away,
And we begin to experience ills.

The longer we live, the more we see,
How precious is this thing called "Time."
It seems life's clock runs faster each day,
And the days seem shorter, each chime.

One generation goes, and another is born,
That is God's plan and design.
No matter how long He lets us live,
We all would ask for more time.

But we must make the days count
Though shorter they seem;
It is easy to become depressed.
But life is precious, and we truly know
That we are abundantly blessed.

So, if our life is long or short,
May we live it true to the end.
For no matter how long, this life is brief,
And quickly comes to an end.

But Eternity waits, where we will never die,
And we'll never have pain or grow old.
But Eternal Springtime, and eternal youth
In that wonderful City of Gold.

MOUNTAINS

Lift your eyes to the hills,
See the mountains so grand,
Observe all the beauty,
Wrought through God's mighty hand.

The Psalmist asked,
From whence cometh my help?
Not from the hills,
But from God, Himself.

The Great God who created
This beauty so grand
Still holds us secure,
In the palm of His hand.

THE FOG

In the still quiet time of the morning
The fog covers the earth with a mist,
Like a drink of water to a thirsty soul,
It's a kiss from God's own lips.

The dry parched leaves from yesterday's sun
Hang heavy, and dusty with heat.
So, the morning mist, and the sparkling dew,
Bring refreshing life so sweet.

Then it is time for the sun to rise in the East,
And the fog must lift away.
It ascends on the clouds,
Where it patiently waits,
To awaken another day.

Mankind like earth, is parched and dry,
In need of a touch from above.
For times of refreshing from God's own hand,
Should be our heart's fervent cry.

CLOUDS

The Lord hath His way in the whirlwind and in the storm,
and the clouds are the dust of His feet.
Nahum 1:3

If the clouds we see are the dust of His feet,
We should never fear or be afraid of defeat.
He is constantly walking, above us God stands,
His feet ever moving, as are the works of His hands.

On a cloudy day, we become depressed,
When it's all the more reason, to see how we're blessed.
For if the dust of His feet, are the clouds we see.
He is keeping close watch, over you and me.

The clouds provide shade and rain, and beauty to see,
What a Wonderful Saviour and Caretaker is He.

When the clouds bring storms we wonder, "Is He
Displeased, as He walks, and our evil sees?"

The clouds bring relief from the heat of the Sun.
He guards and protects us, This Wonderful One.

So, when you look at the Sky,
And see clouds floating and free,
Thank Him for His presence,
Watching over you and me.

LIGHT

When the Moon comes out at night
It plays Hide and Seek, in the clouds,
The Stars gather round, and dance and twinkle;
It seems, they laugh out loud.

They glorify their Maker and King,
The Word says, "For joy they sing."
They move with the Moon all around the sky,
They seem to have such fun;
They play while they may
Till the breaking of Day,
When it is time for the rising Sun.

When the Sun comes out, they fade away,
Its brightness outshines their light;
Old King Sol, is in charge of the Day,
The Moon, and the Stars have the Night.

We like the Moon, can only reflect
The light of the "Risen Son;"
In this darkened world, we are told to shine,
Till He comes, on the wings of the Morn.

The Passing of Time

And that knowing the time, that now is high time to awake out of sleep, for now is our salvation nearer than when we believed.
Romans 13:11

Boast not thyself of tomorrow,
for thou knowest not what a day may bring forth.
Proverbs 27:1

LIFE'S CLOCK

The clock of life is wound but once,
And no one has the power,
To turn it back, and start again,
Not one minute, not one hour.

Our clock may run slow or seem too fast.
But nothing we can do,
Will regain the hours passed,
When Eternity is in view.

Each day when we awaken,
We are blessed with 1440 minutes.
It is up to us, to fill the time,
And choose how we will spend it.

When the Clock of Life has chimed its last,
And the hands of time are stilled,
Live life now, so you won't regret,
How your days on earth were filled.

OUR NUMBERED DAYS

Threescore and ten, we have been told
Are the numbered days of man.
Sometimes they are more, and sometimes less;
Whatever is in God's plan.

We can't add one day to our time allowed,
We can't bargain, or steal, or buy.
We all have an appointed time,
For we know, we all have to die.

How we live, is what matters the most,
For we know this life will end.
So, we must decide, while we are here;
Where our eternal life, we will spend.

LIFE

Life consists of days and time,
And we lose a little with each clock's chime.
So quickly our life passes away,
And we will give an account for every day.

A man's life does not consist,
Of things acquired, or chances he missed.
But the joys he has, and the joy he brings,
Of happiness known, not material things.

This life is not meant for the things we see,
But to prepare our souls for eternity.
Life is wonderful, and is a God-given gift,
We must enjoy each day, for time is so swift.

The beauty of nature, the people we love,
Are precious gifts, from the Father above.
So, live your life knowing, it will soon be o'er.
It is only a Gateway, to where Time is no more.

UNINVITED CHANGE

Have you ever awakened in the morning
To a world that was suddenly strange,
Your surroundings were all familiar,
But everything was completely changed?

For the nighttime crisis had invaded
Your world, where you felt so secure.
And sickness and problems arisen,
And now nothing seemed for sure.

Life is so fleetingly changing,
No promise of tomorrow, we hold.
And our world that seems so comforting,
In a moment, turns lonely and cold.

When sickness and death come to us,
Which sooner or later, we will face.
There is only one thing that will keep us,
And that is God's Mercy, and Grace.

So, we should live our lives knowing
Tomorrow, the picture may change,
And all that we cherish, and live for,
May not be ours to claim.

For God alone knows our future,
Our Times are in His hand.
We must entrust our lives to Him,
Knowing His promises will stand.

FATHER TIME

I went to visit Father Time
To try to learn the truth,
Of why my days were going so fast,
And what had happened to my youth.

He was sitting in front of a door that was closed,
On the front was writing I could not see.
But when I strained to read the words,
They said, "Number of days for...ME."

I asked Father Time what the number was,
He said, "It is behind the door.
Even I don't know, till each day I open,
And one day, there is NO MORE."

Then my mind remembered what the Psalmist said,
That we were to number our days,
And live wisely here, so our life will count,
When our Time on earth, fades away.

TIME

The one thing over we most obsess,
Is something no human can ever possess.
It is not affected by money, or clime,
We will never be owners, of this thing called "Time."

How many times in a day do you suppose
The question of Time, in our minds is posed?
We look at our watch over and over again,
"Do you have the time?" we ask of a friend.

It is time to get up, it is time to eat,
It is time for an appointment, we have to meet.
Our days and our years are measured in time.
Yet, we can never buy it, with dollars or dimes.

The most precious possession in all our life,
Is measured in time, counted by days, and nights.
We ask over and over, the time of the day,
All is measured in time, our work and our play.

We build our lives and plan our days
On what the hands of the clock have to say.
Something we cannot touch or control.
Has power over our life, and our soul.

We cannot control the clouds or the wind,
We can only receive what God chooses to send.
'NOW' is all the time we possess,
Use it wisely, knowing, it is because God has blessed.

LIFE'S VOYAGE

We are all a sail on the Sea of Time
In a boat that is all our own.
Some are small crafts with room for only a few;
While others are luxury liners that carry crowds
And cross the Ocean blue.

Some spend their days on a small fishing lake,
And others stay close to the shore;
But they all have a destiny they have to meet
Before they finally moor.

Some boats are for pleasure and fun and ease,
And others work hard all day toiling the open seas.
Some are powered by wind, and others by oars,
Never moving far from land and shore.

While others travel the breadth of the mighty seas,
With powerful engines, they move with great ease.
Some voyages are long, and others are brief;
But all have a Port, and a destiny to meet.

The ones who land safely at the end of their sail,
Are those who have Jesus as Captain,
For He guides them safely
Through life's stormy gales.

HE GETS OUR ATTENTION

We hurry and rush, and worry, and stew
And think of all we have to do;
We think all of our plans we have to fulfill
And we never have time, to just be still.

So sometimes God has to intervene
And change our plans, when He comes on the scene.
Sometimes He uses sickness to slacken our pace,
Sometimes He does it, with the tiny snowflakes.

Our jobs and activities we think have to be;
But sometimes God says, "Take time for Me."
What part in your life do you allow Him to claim,
Do you think of eternity, or just earthly fame?

He covers the ground with a blanket of white
And man has to acknowledge His power and might.
Nature bows to His will, and man can see;
How helpless and hopeless alone, he would be.

When we see the snow and its beautiful drifts,
We are reminded of God's wonderful gift.
His only Son, Jesus, who died in our stead.
To wash us whiter than snow,
In His Blood that He shed.

THE CALENDAR

Last year's Calendar is a record of events,
Of appointments we made, and the places we went.
Some dates were circled as a Red-Letter Day.
Others are marked, with a bill, due to pay.

Looking back through the calendar, of all that is past,
We are reminded that Time goes so fast.
We see days of happiness, and some days of sorrow.
But they are all now "yesterday,"
There are no tomorrows.

What we did, where we went,
And whatever the weather;
Are past history now, they are days gone forever.
There is no returning to the days of last year;
It seems but a moment, that the first day appeared.

So, we hang the New Calendar with its pages so clean,
What the days ahead hold, is unknown and unseen.
The days seem each year to quicken their pace,
And each day we live, is a gift of God's Grace.

So, fill your calendar with Eternity in view,
And with God's help, you will make it through.
When the year has ended, and thrown out as the "past,"
May its days show recorded the deeds that will last.

Our hearts are always with what we hold treasured;
Plan your calendar to count, where Time is not measured.
Earth's Calendars are useless on Eternity's shore,
Where there is neither day nor night,
For Time is no more.

Celebrations & Holidays
and remembering Christ's Birth and Sacrificial Death for us

*This is the day which the L*ORD* hath made;*
we will rejoice and be glad in it.
Psalm 118:24

WOULD YOU HAVE HELPED?

If you had been in Jerusalem that day
When they took the Saviour and led Him away,
If you could have been among the throng,
When He took up the Cross, and walked alone,

When He stumbled and fell on the Calvary Road,
Would you have said to Him, "Let me carry the load,
For your back is bleeding, and your strength is gone,
Give me the Cross, let me walk along?"

When you saw them strike Him, and slap His face,
Would you have said, "Here, hit me in His place?"
When the cat o' nine tails lashed on His bare skin,
Would you have said, "Hit me, I'm the one who has sinned?"

We think had we been there we would have tried
To do something to help Him, not just watch as He died.
But today, when we can, do we stand in His place?
Do we show His love? Do we tell of His Grace?

When His name is blasphemed, and His Gospel denied,
Do we stand up for Jesus, or try to hide?
Are we like the throng on the Calvary Road,
Letting Jesus alone, carry the load?

We have a chance now to lift high the Cross,
To share Salvation to a world that is lost.

WHO WAS IN THE MANGER?

Who was in the manger that night in Bethlehem?
It was a Shepherd, a Priest, a Prophet, a Lamb.
Who was in the manger, nestled in the straw?
It was the God of Glory, the lowly shepherds saw.

Who was in the manger, lying helpless as a babe?
It was the Blessed Son of God,
by whom all things were made.

Who was in the manger the shepherds came to see?
It was the spotless Lamb of God
they worshipped on their knees.

Who was in the manger that night so long ago?
'Twas He who spoke into existence
all things that we now know.
It was God Omnipotent, full of Glory and Grace
That came to earth as a baby, in such a lowly place.

He made the wood for the manger
Where He lay his head, when He came as a stranger.
All things were made by Him, and nothing was made,
Except by decree from that tiny babe.

Who was in the manger? I'm glad we know the One,
Who came to earth an infant and born as God's dear Son.
I am glad He is no longer a helpless babe upon the hay,
But He is Almighty God, ruling and reigning today.

It isn't the Christ of the manger,
but the Christ of Calvary's cross,
Where He paid for our sins, Gave us new life in Him.
So, all who believe, and His life receive,
Will never, ever, be lost.

MALCHUS

When Malchus went home from the Garden,
He was still shaking with wonder and fear.
His wife asked what was the matter,
And he told her about his ear.

She said, "I don't believe you;
Your ear looks perfectly fine.
I thought you said you were working,
And you come home drunk on wine."

Malchus said, "I have not been drinking,
I was, as I said, at work.
If you don't believe my story,
Look at the blood on my shirt."

Our job was arresting this Jesus;
One of His Own, turned Him in.
The One who goes about teaching,
And claims He can forgive sin.

We were about ready to take Him
When one disciple got mad.
He said, "You will not arrest Him."
And I saw the sword that he had.

He was swinging it around so wildly,
I thought someone would die.
And then he raised the sword toward me,
And my ear, on the ground, I saw lie.

It all happened so quickly,
Then I felt the pain in my ear.
But the One we had been arresting,
Said, "Malchus, come over here."

He rebuked the one who had cut me;
Told him to put the sword away.
He said, "I will go with the Soldiers,
I have come to Earth, for this day."

Then I felt His hand, so gently,
Just a tender touch on my ear.
When I felt where it had been severed,
It was just as you see here.

When He was touching my ear so quickly,
His eyes seemed to pierce my soul.
He said not a word to me,
But my ear was made perfectly whole.

I am sure that Malchus followed
The crowd up Calvary's Hill.
As he watched while the crosses were lifted,
His heart must have stood still.

He pondered all he had witnessed
And the events he had seen and heard.
He looked as Jesus was dying,
And was aware of His final words.

Jesus said, "Father forgive them,
For they know not what they do."
As Malchus's hand raised to his ear,
He knew this Jesus, was true.

We are not told in the Scripture
If Salvation, Malchus received.
I'd like to think, as he stood there,
In his heart, he truly believed.

WHY THE STABLE?

When God came to earth in human form,
He could have chosen a palace for His Son to be born.
Royal attendants could have served at the birth,
The attending physician could have been the finest on Earth.

Trumpets could have sounded,
With the royal banner unfurled,
Announcing the good news
The Lord of Glory had come to the world.

But God didn't choose a palace, or a place of great fame,
He chose a lowly stable, and only poor Shepherds came.

The Mightiest King who would ever be born,
Arrived in a stable on that first Christmas morn.
Mary, and Joseph, and Jesus made three,
That is all who were present, when the Shepherds came to see.

God chose the stable and the manger bed,
And even when older, He had no place to lay His head.
Shepherds and wise men, came from afar
Guided to Jesus, by the bright shining star.

To the lowly Shepherds the Angels appeared
Announcing the birth of the Saviour,
And quieting their fears.

He was born in a stable, so all men would know,
He is the Saviour of all men,
No matter how low.

THE FATHER'S GIFT

When we envision Christmas, we think of the Manger scene.
We think of Mary and Joseph, and we hear the Angels sing.
But there's another part of the Story,
and it is the Father in Heaven above.
Who sent His Son to Earth, to prove His infinite love.

He knew what His Son would suffer;
He knew how abused He would be.
Yet He permitted this all to happen
because He so loved you and me.

When our children leave home, we miss them;
We pass by their bedroom door,
We wish they were still small children,
And we could have them home once more.

Now, the Heavenly Throne is half empty,
Occupied by the Father alone.
The Son's place, where He sat beside Him,
Is empty now that He's gone.

A day is as a thousand years.
And a thousand years as a day.
We know that Time is not measured in Heaven,
But think, how long it seemed He was away.

So, when you think of that first Christmas morning,
How Jesus willingly came.
Remember how hard for His Father,
To send Him to such sorrow and shame.

We say Christmas is all about Jesus
And we know, He and The Father, are One.
So, give thanks to our Father in Heaven;
For the gift of His Wonderful Son.

CHRISTMAS PAST

When I think of Christmases past
Christmas in the days long ago;
It seemed the days were long and cold.
And it almost always snowed.

The tree was just a scraggly pine
With homemade bows and chains,
Made from colored paper, and flour paste,
And popcorn on a string.

Most of the time, there were no lights,
But strands of tinsel shined;
Hung on the tree, year after year,
Always saved for another time.

Then later on, when I was grown,
And had children of my own,
The tree was still a scraggly pine,
But decorated with ornaments bought,
And lights to make it shine.

There were always toys to fulfill a wish,
Some bought from the Dollar Store,
But we always managed to grant one wish,
And they never asked for more.

But they left home, and the house was quiet,
Christmas Eve, just another day.
No more toys to construct in the night,
No small children to run and play.

But Christmas Day brought them home again,
And the house was filled once more.
Grandchildren gathered around the tree,
For they knew what was in store.

Then they grew older, and once again,
Christmas was never the same.
No noisy shouts and yells of glee
No plastic toys, or games.

But money gifts or perhaps clothes to wear,
Practical gifts were the thought.
No children to play, or scream with delight,
To See what Santa had brought.

But Christmas will always be Christmas,
though the years of time will bring change.
We will always have memories of Christmases past,
The love of Christmas will always remain.

THE MANGER AND THE CROSS

The tiny babe in the manger
Could not save a world that was lost.
He had to become a man,
And die on Calvary's Cross.

He had to suffer temptation
And know what it was to be a man;
To be the Perfect Redeemer,
It was all part of God's Sovereign plan.

He was tempted, as we are tempted,
He knew pain, and sorrow, and woe.
He was born in Bethlehem's manger,
But to Calvary's Cross, He would go.

Bethlehem's manger would be useless
If the Cross was not in the plan,
Not His birth, but His sufferings at Calvary,
To become sacrifice, for fallen man.

He was wounded for our transgressions,
He was bruised for our awful sins,
The crown of thorns and His beatings,
He endured, our Redemption to win.

The tomb where they placed Him was borrowed,
It was only needed three days.
For the Angel told Mary, and those with her.
"Come see the place where He lay."

They saw only the place, not the body,
For Resurrection morning had come.
He now is ascended to Heaven.
Where He intercedes for us at God's Throne.

THE UNCLAIMED GIFT

I bought a gift for an old-time friend,
And placed it lovingly under the tree.
It had been so long, since we shared good times,
I was glad he was visiting me.

Then Christmas came, and the holidays passed,
And he didn't come or call.
It seemed the friendship held so dear,
To him, didn't matter at all.

One day while looking on the closet shelf,
I saw the Christmas gift.
Still wrapped in paper, now dirty and torn,
My friend's name on the unclaimed gift.

I thought of another, who purchased a gift,
And the price He paid was high.
When God sent His Son, to a sin cursed earth,
To a cross, where He knew He would die.

Tremendous in sacrifice, so high was the cost,
Providing Salvation, to a world that was lost.
God sent His Son, to mankind on earth,
Sent Him by way of the virgin birth.

With such a price paid, it would not be expected,
This gift be unclaimed, and this love be rejected.
The Gift of Salvation purchased on the Cross blood stained,
Like my gift to my friend, is ignored and unclaimed.

The name on this gift purchased with Blood:
"Whosoever will come" and receive His love.
He took all our sins and carried our shame.
This Gift of Salvation, is ours, free to claim.

NOVEMBER

November's skies are often grey.
The summer has ended,
And short are the days.

The year's end approaches;
How quickly it seems,
The sunshine of summer,
Is only a dream.

November is a time
To reflect in our thoughts,
Of the good things in life,
This past year has brought.

We are made aware,
At this time of Thanksgiving,
How God graced us, and blessed us,
In our daily living.

CHRISTMAS

When Christmas Day is over,
And the decorations taken down,
The house takes on a different mood,
It seems there is not a sound.

When the lights are all aglow
And Christmas music is in the air,
The days go by so quickly,
No one seems to have a care.

Then workdays come, and off we go,
To our plans and different ways.
It makes us wish that every day
Could be like Christmas Day.

But the hustle and the bustle
Of the daily life takes hold,
And so quickly we forget the joy
Of hearing the Christmas story told.

But just because the calendar changes
And we have different jobs to do,
We should strive to keep the Spirit of Christmas
In our lives the whole year through.

GOD'S PERFECT GIFT

Sometimes as a child at Christmas time,
I'd wait for the day when the house was mine.
Mom was gone shopping, and I was by myself;
So, I would look in the closet, and on the top shelf;
Hoping to find my Christmas gift hidden away,
Waiting to surprise me on Christmas Day.

The anticipation was more than I could bear,
So, to look better, I would stand on a chair;
There it was, wrapped so pretty and neat,
But I knew I had to have a peek.
So, carefully I would undo the tape,
Peek inside the box 'cause I couldn't wait.

Just what I wanted I shouted with glee;
Mom always knew just how to please me.
But I will have to open with expectant eyes,
And not let Mom know and spoil her surprise.

The Greatest Gift ever given to me
Was not put under, but hung on a tree.
God gave this gift on Calvary's cross,
Salvation free, though priceless the cost.

We can't see this Gift which we know we'll receive,
For it is promised to all who truly believe.
Our minds can't imagine the splendor and bliss
That awaits us in Heaven, God's perfect gift.

If you want a preview look,
Open the pages of God's wonderful Book.
Eye has not seen, nor has ear heard,
But the treasures awaiting us are described in His Word.

CHRISTMAS RED AND GREEN

Why do we wear red at Christmas
And have "hanging of the greens?"
If you know the meaning of Christmas
The answer is clearly seen.

Christmas is all about Jesus:
How He came to earth for man.
It was God showing love to a sin cursed earth,
All part of His Sovereign plan.

So, the RED we wear at Christmas
Makes us think of His Holy Blood.
Shed on the Cross, as He died that day,
It still has power, after all this time,
To wash every sin away.

The EVERGREEN TREE is the symbol of life,
For its colors never fade.
It speaks of His Word, which will never fail,
though heaven and earth pass away.

The RED and GREEN at Christmas
Are special to us who believe,
And open our hearts at Christmas time,
His wonderful gift to receive.

So, when you tie a red bow
Or put lights on an evergreen tree,
Thank God for His gift to the world,
Salvation, though priceless, is free.

THE CANDLES OF THE CHRISTMAS SPIRIT

Written for a children's program.

The Christmas Spirit is all around.
In every heart it does abound.
I light this candle which burns to show,
Christmas, today, is the same as two thousand years ago.
The Christmas Spirit should fill our minds with thoughts of Him
Who was born long ago, as the Saviour of men.
If giving is foremost in our thoughts,
Let's begin by giving him our hearts.

THE CANDLE OF LOVE

This candle burns as the star of LOVE.
it shines on earth from God above.
As the "Star of the East" it is better known,
but it was God's love shining from His throne.
It led three wise men to worship the King;
It made the Shepherds rejoice and sing.
They were guided to Bethlehem by the light of the Star;
The Star of God's love shines wherever you are.

THE CANDLE OF PEACE

PEACE is the symbol of this candle I light,
Peace that was shed abroad in the hearts of men that night.
The angels sang peace to the shepherds on the hills;
The peace of God to them was made real.
God made a covenant of peace with man,
For the blood of Jesus, the gulf did span.
We have peace with God through our Lord Jesus Christ
Who was born in Judea, that first Christmas night.

THE CANDLE OF GUIDANCE

This candle burns as the guiding Star.
That led the wise men on their journey far.
The Blessed Messiah at last was here,
The star was guiding them to the child so dear.

This candle burns as the star did that night,
Leading the wise men with an unfaltering light.
It led them to the child so Holy,
Born in a stable, so meek and lowly.

THE CANDLE OF HOPE

This candle burns as a testimony of HOPE in the Lord
For our hope is in Him and our trust is in His Word.
I wish for you this Christmas night
That in your soul the light of hope burns bright.
Without "Christ in you, the Hope of Glory"
There would be no need for the Christmas story.
For Jesus was born to dwell in the hearts of men
To save their souls, and cleanse from sin.

THE CANDLE OF JOY

This candle burns as a symbol of JOY
That was given by the birth of a tiny baby boy.
Jesus brought joy that night in Bethlehem,
And the same joy still reigns in the hearts of men.
The angels sang of goodwill and joy
As they announced the birth of the baby boy!
Jesus was born, the angels did sing,
A song of joy, of the Saviour and King.

THE CANDLE OF FAITH

This candle burns as the light of FAITH.
Faith in Jesus who took our place.
He was born long ago in the City of David,
And with hearts of faith, we claim Him as our Saviour.
As this candle burns with a light true and bright,
May our faith so shine in Jesus, who is love's pure light.
May our light of faith cast its beams far and wide
Until we tell the world of sinners for them Jesus died.

WHY THE SHEPHERDS?

Do you ever wonder why the shepherds
Were the first mortals God chose to tell,
That He had come to earth as an infant
Among them to live and to dwell?

The shepherds of lowly profession lived in caves with the sheep.
They spent days and nights in the desert; not even a bed for sleep.
Away from the crowded cities their lot was lonely and bleak;
Sometimes their only conversation
Was met with the bleat of a sheep.

But God, being the Great Shepherd, knew what it was to love sheep;
That is why He instructed His children to be as He is, lowly and meek.
On earth He knew no great riches; He had no place to sleep.
He was as the earthly Shepherd tending His chosen sheep.

The ones keeping watch in the fields
Were chosen that first Christmas night;
The watchful and faithful shepherd
To see His star shine so bright.

God knew His people, like sheep would need special love and care;
That is why He sent hosts of angels this wonderful news to share.
He said He is meek and lowly; no respecter of persons is He,
The kings in the royal cities were not chosen this light to see.

But the poor, and the lost, and the lonely,
Are the ones He came to earth to redeem;
That is why the Shepherds were chosen
To witness the world's greatest scene.

THE SPEAKING STONE AT THE SEPULCHRE

When they placed Jesus in the tomb, Pilate was heard to say,
Make fast the entrance, so no one can steal Him away.
So, they placed a stone across the door, and put Sentries all around.

The Sentries said, "For this they pay,
To guard the tomb where a dead man lay?
Don't they know we are prison guards,
Our work tonight will not be hard."

So, they joked and laughed about standing guard,
They said, "Boy, this is really hard.
What does Pilate think a dead man can do?
Why, we can sleep the whole night through.
The stone at the door must weigh a ton,
What does he think, can a dead man run?
We are used to hard work, but this is 'too much!'
We can't believe Pilate is making such a fuss."

But as the night grew still the guards thought they heard
Someone speaking, but they knew not the words.
The stone at the door was heard to shout,
"Jesus, I know you are coming out!"

For these men won't praise you, so I must cry and shout,
Move over Guards, for He is coming out.
I see an Angel coming this way, see, I'm rolling back,
IT'S RESURRECTION DAY!

When the morning broke thru the gloom,
And Pilate checked on the guards at the tomb,
They were as dead men on the ground
And the body of Jesus was not to be found.
Pilate kept hearing the strangest sound.
The rocks were all crying from the ground,
"Our Creator is risen, He is not here!"
And Pilate left, trembling, and filled with fear.

ACROSTIC OF "CHRISTMAS"

CHRIST was born that Christmas night,
Clad in clothes of celestial light.
Born within the City of David, proves He is the Promised Saviour
He was once a baby small; now He is the Lord Of All.
Crown Him with a diadem,
for He was born in Bethlehem.

HARK, THE HERALD ANGELS sing!
These good tidings, angels bring.
Christ is born this Holy day; come with us to watch and pray.
He was born this Christmas night; the Son of God, loves pure light.
Leading those who are astray,
H is for this Holy Day.

ROYAL RICHES had He none,
Though He was God's chosen Son.
In a manger filled with hay, Christ was born on Christmas Day.
No room left, the Inn Keeper said; a straw-filled manger was his bed.
Make sure you have room for Him today;
Don't turn Him away.

IN THE INN there was no bed
On which the Christ Child lay his head.
In the manger filled with hay, blessed Baby Jesus lay.
Now unto the King, Eternal, Immortal,
The only wise God, be honor and glory.
We make a place this Christmas night,
In our hearts, for love's pure light.

SUCH A WONDROUS GIFT was given
When our Saviour came from Heaven
The One who is our light and life, was such a tiny babe that night.
No longer is He in the manger, no longer is He to us a stranger.
He is our Lord and Mighty King. This is what our Christmas means.

TRIMMING THE TREE and hanging holly
The time of year when everyone is jolly.
Let us not forget in our minds today, that Christmas is a Holy Day.
For on this day, God gave His Son, to die on the cross for everyone.
The greatest gift that ever was given,
When God gave His Son to us from Heaven.

MULTITUDES sang in the Heavenly choir
Praising God and giving Him glory,
For the Word was made flesh, to dwell among men
That promised night in Bethlehem.
Mighty and Merciful is He that came down
From His throne in Heaven, to a thorny crown.
He was born to die, that we might live,
What a great Christmas present, God chose to give.

ANGELS FILLED THE SKY that night
To tell about the star so bright,
That hung over a stable in Bethlehem,
where inside was born the Saviour of men.
A choir of Angels sang that glad story
Of the birth of the Son of God so Holy.
Today, we tell the story anew,
How the Promised Saviour came to you.

SHEPERDS SAW the same bright star
That led the wise men from afar,
Led them where the Christ Child lay, in a manger filled with hay.
Today we need no star above, to tell about His wondrous love.
Love was shown in God's great gift
To all men, that first Christmas.

THE THREE CROSSES

On the day that Jesus was crucified
There were two other crosses, one on each side.

Two thieves were to die with Jesus that day,
One of them cursed, while the other, would pray.

He said, "This man is just, He should be free.
Jesus, when you come to Your Kingdom, please remember me."

Jesus assured him he would not be lost,
For his Salvation was purchased there on the middle cross.

We, like the thief, will never be lost,
If we believe on the Christ of the middle cross.

WHO WAS BARABBAS?

Barabbas sat in his cell that day,
Waiting for the guards to take him away.
He was a rioter, a murderer, a robber, a thief,
Of hardened criminals, he surely was chief.

But who was Barabbas, this creature so low,
If he did so much wrong, then why could he go?
He was a rioter, a thief, a killer of man,
The blood of his neighbor, dripped from his hand.

But the crowd in Pilate's Hall was heard to say,
"Free Barabbas, let him go on his way."
We care not if he's guilty, just let him go free.
It's the death of this 'JESUS' we want to see.

But who was Barabbas, they freed that day?
Let's read in Corinthians, what Paul had to say,
"Revilers, extortioners, drunkards, and thieves,
Into Heaven, will not be received."

But who is Paul speaking about,
Read on in the verse, and you will find out.
"And such were you, the same as Barabbas so low,
Before you were washed in Calvary's flow."

So, WE were Barabbas, who was freed that day,
When they crucified Jesus and sent us on our way.
For He took our judgment and died in our place.
We were Barabbas, who was freed by Grace.

AND THEY STRIPPED HIM
Matthew 27:28

When they led Jesus to Golgotha's Hill
Where the old rugged cross, stood straight and still,
It wasn't enough that He suffered such pain,
They wanted to put Him to open shame.

So, they stripped Him of his garments, and smote his face,
Though his GARMENTS were gone, He was still clothed in GRACE.
Grace that would comfort and save you and me,
Grace that would pardon and let us go free.

They stripped Him of His robe that He wore on that day,
But He was still a King; they couldn't take that away.
His ROYALTY lies not in the ROBE that was blood stained,
He is still King of kings, in His eternal REIGN.

They took his CLOTHING, and cast it away,
But his COMPASSION He kept, as He humbly prayed.
His compassionate heart they couldn't control,
Even as they stripped Him, He prayed for their soul.

They took his RAIMENT in that awful hour,
But they couldn't take his REDEMPTIVE POWER.
He was still God Almighty, though dying as man,
Though naked and stripped, He was Salvation's plan.

They took his APPAREL, and mocked Him to scorn,
They placed on His head, a crown of thorns.
They said, "King of the Jews" He claims to be,
But His omnipotent AUTHORITY, they soon would see.

Though His APPAREL was gone,
And He was shamed and disgraced,
He would lay down His life, and His life, again take.
For His AUTHORITY remained, and His omnipotent power,
They soon would see, in His resurrection hour.

They stripped His VESTURE as He was nailed to the cross,
They gambled to see, who won, and who lost.
Though His VESTURE they took, and He hung there in shame;
They couldn't take the VICTORY, that was His to claim.

He rose in great victory, over death and the grave,
And this victory belongs to all who are saved,
For He is the First Fruits of that Resurrection Hour.
Though they stripped Him and mocked Him,
He's still the God of all power.

FROM PRISON TO PARADISE BY THE WAY OF THE CROSS

The Prison doors opened on that fateful day,
The guard appeared, led two prisoners away.
"Judgment time is here, crucifixion you will see."
"We are only two, we thought there were three."

One prisoner said, "Where is the other one?
We heard He claims to be God's Son."
"Move on, it is time," the guard replies,
"What difference does it make? You are going to die."

As they climb the hill where the crosses await,
Scared and shaking to meet their fate,
Three crosses were there with soldiers around,
Waiting to drop them into the ground.

The Man in the middle, cried, "Father, forgive."
One of the thieves said, "I want to live."
He said, "Lord, I believe you are God's Son.
Remember me, when to your Kingdom you come."

A mighty miracle happened right then,
Jesus forgave him for all of his sin.
"Today" He said, "In Paradise with me,
When you draw your last breath, that is where you will be."

From Prison to Paradise, by way of the Cross
By trusting Jesus, to save him from loss.
What a miracle of love was seen that day,
When Jesus answered the thief who would pray.

He left Prison that morning with his head bowed low,
Then entered Paradise, washed in Calvary's flow.

BETRAYAL

When Jesus was led from the Garden He went with the Guards, alone.
Not one disciple went with Him, they had all forsaken and run.
Then Peter decided to follow, and went thru the courtyard gate.
He thought he would warm by the fire pit,
And learn what would be Jesus' fate.

As he stood by the fire, someone spied him,
And said, "You are one of the clan."
Dropping his eyes, Peter murmured,
"What you are saying, I don't understand."
Then another said, "Listen! His speech just gave him away!"
Again, Peter murmured softly, "I don't know the man, as you say."

Then the third accuser approached him,
Said, "Deny the truth, if you dare."
Frightened, and trembling Peter answered,
"I know Him not," with a curse and a swear.
Then Peter heard In the darkness the sound of the rooster's crow.
And the realization hit him, what Jesus had told him, was so.

When the door of the Judgment Hall opened,
And Jesus came through the crowd,
In the glow of the fire, He saw Peter,
But He spoke not a word out loud.

His face was bruised and bleeding; His back was torn in shreds.
Peter saw the look in His eyes, but no hatred, or malice, he read.
Peter knew Jesus would forgive him,
But oh, the pain of it all.
If he had it all to do over,
He'd go with Him to Caiaphas' Hall.

When we fail to uphold our Saviour,
And we have a chance to do right,
If by our silence, we deny Him,
We are the same as Peter that night.

CALVARY

When God looked down from Heaven's Throne,
And saw His Son covered, in sins, not His own.
He turned His back, and hid His face,
Too Holy to look on such sin and disgrace.

All alone, Jesus cried in agony,
"Father, why hast Thou forsaken me?"
But God remained silent, left Jesus to die,
Shutting His ears to His Only Son's cry.

God is light, in Him is no darkness at all.
If He remained present, no darkness could fall.
For three long hours utter darkness remained,
As Jesus gave His life's blood, to cleanse every stain.

When Jesus cried, "It is finished, the work is now done.
I have accomplished the mission for which I have come,"
Then the darkness was over, God's wrath was appeased,
With His Son's sacrifice, He was well pleased.

Never again would His Son be alone.
At the Father's right hand, He is seated on the Throne,
Making intercession for all who have believed,
In what He wrought at the Cross, and His Atonement, received.

THE FATHER'S VALENTINE

A father loves his children, each and every one;
But there is a special place within his heart, for his one and only Son.
When the children all leave home, the house is not the same.
Silence fills the rooms where the children's laughter rang.

In the Eons of Eternity, God the Father and the Son,
Had never been apart, for they are made as One.
In all the vast eternities, only thirty-three short years;
Would Jesus leave the Father and as a Babe, on Earth appear.

God the Father sent a Valentine to Earth
A Blood red present from His heart,
His Son, through virgin birth.

This Valentine was given from the Heavenly Father's love.
He said, "Bring to Me a family, to live with Us above."
Heaven's halls were not the same while Jesus was not there;
The Seat beside the Father on the Heavenly Throne was bare.

When God told Abraham to sacrifice his son
In the heart of Abraham, the awful deed was done.
So, in God's heart, His Son was dead
Crucified on the Cross, so blood-stained Red.

This Valentine sent, as the Baby's birth
Was prepared and sacrificed
Before God made the Earth.

God sends to you, this Valentine
Written in Red, saying, "Will you be Mine?"
And as the earthly father is glad when his children return home,
God and Jesus wait together, for the day His children come.

THE NEW YEAR

The New Year that lies before us, with things we cannot see;
The paths that we must take, and things that are meant to be;
Some will go merrily onward, with mountains of joy to scale,
And others will mournfully walk,
Through shadows and darkness of Vales.

The unknown year before us, is a journey we all must make,
And none of us know the future; what paths will be ours to take.
How far on this journey we travel, is also a mystery too;
Some will see only a portion, while others go all the year through.

For some, the year will be happy,
Filled with joy, and laughter, and ease.
With never a fretful moment, or nothing that seems to displease.
But others will struggle and suffer, and each day seem so unfair;
They wonder why they keep going,
When life is ought but more care.

If we could choose the path, that all of us would walk.
We all would choose the sunshine, no one would be in the dark.
There would be no pain or sorrow, no one would suffer loss.
Life would always be laughter and joy; no one would carry a cross.

But God will choose our pathway, as into this year we go,
And He will lead us onward, into the future, that only He knows.
So, we must trust our Father with this New Year that we face.
And lean on His arms, and trust in His love,
And we'll make it through by His Grace.

THE NEW YEAR

A lot of things happened in the year just gone by,
Many things occurred, that made us ask, Why?
But the world goes on, as is God's plan
We still are held in His Mighty hand.

Every day this past year the Sun arose,
Bathing Earth with a golden glow.
Each night that followed, saw the stars still shine,
Their majesty proclaiming God's perfect design.

The Oceans still stop at the beaches of sand,
That God decreed as a boundary for land.
The winds still blow, and the storms arise,
All under the care of God's watchful eye.

All of Nature declares that God still reigns.
He is the Keeper of earth, and all its domain.
The heavens declare God's Glory and Might
While the firmament shows His work with delight.

In all He created, and in all of His plan,
The only rebellion is in sinful man.
Nature acknowledges that God is in control,
Man alone, strives to master his soul.

If we will submit to the All Sovereign One,
Accept His Salvation, through the death of His Son.
The year ahead will be free from fear.
For His guidance and love, will always be near.

THE "ABCs" OF THANKFULNESS

Thank you, God, for the AIR we breathe,
And for all the BLESSINGS from your hand we receive.
Thank you for CONSOLATION when we are in pain.
And for every refreshing DROP OF RAIN.

Thank You for being Your ETERNAL EXISTING SELF,
And for all our FOOD on our pantry shelf.
Thank you for GRACE provided for every day,
And for HEALTH to work and make our way.

Thank you for INVITING us to share,
And for the JOY we find in daily prayer.
Thank you for your KEEPING POWER,
And for LOVE that remains in life's dark hours.

Thank you for your MERCY great,
and for NEVER turning us away.
Thank you for your OPEN ARMS,
That keeps and PROTECTS us from all harm.

Thank you, God for QUIET HOURS,
And for REDEMPTION wrought by your power.
Thank you for SALVATION'S PLAN
For TRUTH that pardons and liberates man.

Thank you for the UNCTION we receive
For VICTORY that is ours, when we believe.
Thank you for being so WONDERFUL, and WISE,
For our EXPECTATION, that one day, we will rise.

Thank you for your YOKE that is easy to bear,
That keeps us looking for You to appear.
Then the ZENITH of all we are thankful for,
When we behold Your face, on Heaven's bright shore.

Family & Friendship

A friend loveth at all times.
Proverbs 17:17a

A MOTHER AND A SON

Some things in life are easy to explain
Summer always follows Winter, and sunshine follows rain.
But there are some things in life we ponder,
And never seem to know,
We share our happy thoughts and hide our secret woes.

A mother and a daughter share the bond of womanhood.
And most of the time, their relationship is good.
But between a mother and a son, it is hard to explain;
For when he reaches manhood, he feels he has to change.

When he was a little boy, he would run to mother's arms,
But now that he's a man, he faces up to life's harms.
He thinks it is unmanly, to weep on mother's shoulders,
And he cannot show his feelings, now that he is older.

But if he could only see, inside his mother's breast.
Her heart still knows, when her son is facing life's distress.
A daughter will confide, let her feelings be made known,
But a son thinks it is his duty, to bear his load alone.

To our sons, we mothers would like to make them know
That we are always here for them, no matter where they go.
We want them to be strong, to face life like a man,
But we hurt, when they hurt, and our hearts still understand.

Today, so many sons are out of reach of mother's hand,
Some in foreign countries, some in barren desert lands.
Some are facing wars and dangers, things beyond control;
May they know that mother's praying, for the safety of their soul.

So, to the sons now grown, maybe gone or still nearby
May you know that you will always be your mother's heart cry.
She knows you have to stand, have to face life's sorrow and joy;
The man you are, makes her proud,
But you will always be her boy.

MOTHER

M
is for the many ways you gave yourself to me.
O
is for the overshadowing example I could always see.
T
is for the trust and tender care and trueness of your life.
H
Is for the home you made, to shelter us from strife.
E
Is for endurance, and example, by which you taught.
R
Is for riches in Heaven, your life here has wrought.

EVE

When Eve was taken from Adam's side,
And brought to him to be his bride.
She could not have known what she was giving,
When God said, "Eve, you're the mother of all living."

When the time of the birth of a baby nears,
Our hearts are filled with wonder and fear,
Will we be blessed with a baby boy,
Who will fill our lives with pride and joy?
Or will the baby be a sweet little girl,
With dimpled chin, and golden curls?

When a little girl comes into our arms
Our hearts are won by her innocent charm.
All dads want a boy, their image to be,
One they say, "Will be just like me."
But there is something about a girl and her dad;
He never could wish she had been a lad.

Then our little girl grows and matures in her life,
And before we know it, she has become a wife.
It's hard to believe how the years have flown,
And surely, Little Eve, couldn't be grown.
So, we watch her start her journey in life,
On her wedding day, a beautiful Bride.
We wish her the best, but our hearts well know,
Some things in life through which she will go.

Then once again, our little Eve,
Another role in life, is about to receive.
For one day she says, with her face all aglow,
There is something, Mom and Dad,
I want you to know.

And we know before she can say it aloud,
And never before have we been so proud.
For God's plan through Eve is still at work,
For we are awaiting our grandchild's birth.

So, when the day of the birth appears,
Our daughter gives birth, to a baby girl dear.
Now she will assume the role of mother,
And raise her family as before have others.

The years go by and the family increases,
But still God's law, through Eve, He is keeping.
Our granddaughter, now grown, married, and she,
Has now become, a mother-to-be.
And the cycle goes on and is understood
As what we know, as Motherhood,

From Eve in the garden, Adam's wife,
God began a beautiful life.
So, each time a little girl is given,
We see again EVE, the Mother of all living

WHAT IS A MOTHER?

What is a mother?
If you asked a child today,
You would probably be surprised
At the answer they would say.
They would say, "She is the one,
Who takes me to my games,
So I can have my fun."

"She takes me to McDonalds,
She takes me to the mall,
She takes me to my friends,
So we can play ball.
She keeps my room all clean,
She washes all my clothes.
She never makes me do a thing,
That's why I love her so."

Such a far cry from the Mothers,
That we knew some years ago.
Who knew that work and discipline,
Was what made the children grow.

The mothers that we knew,
Spent more time with frying pan,
Than the mothers of today,
We find in mini-vans.

The mothers that we knew
Were mostly found at home.
When we returned from school,
Asked us how we had done.

Our meals were cooked at home,
no greasy fast fried foods,
But meals so lovingly prepared,
So tasty and so good.

Today's mothers are so different,
Than they were long ago.
But there is one thing,
That is still the same.
That is "Mother's Love" they show.

They live a different style
Than we did in days gone by,
But the children now, as then,
Are still the apple of her eye.

One thing that never changes,
Is a faithful mother's love.
It is a gift to all her children,
From our Father, up above.

God gave us earthly mothers
To portray His love on earth
That no matter where we go,
We are His, by right of birth.

A mother's love is changeless,
No matter what we do,
She will always be there for us,
And her love will still be true.

FRIENDSHIP

Friendship is a bond that is formed between our hearts,
And stays there through all our lives, whether near or far apart.
So many years have passed and so many changes taken place,
Since first we met so long ago, with our future yet to face.

We were young and strong
With small children at our feet,
We were filled with dreams and passions;
Health was good, and life was sweet.

There were camping trips and picnics;
Life was laughter, joy, and vim.
Now our eyesight seems to fade,
And our hearing seems to dim.

Never in our wildest dreams did we imagine
The turns and curves life's road would take.
We would meet with trials and heartaches
Endured only through God's Love and Grace.

Some have tasted heartaches too deep to even share;
Some have dealt with death and sickness,
That seems more than one could bear.
But we never lost our hope, for God's promises are true,
He has guided every step, and He will see us through.

So, as you face the unknown future,
Don't be filled with fear and dread.
This life is only temporal,
And the Best is yet ahead.

FRIENDSHIP

Friendship's chain has many links,
It grows throughout the years.
Our hearts are knit in kindred ties,
And time makes them more dear.

The strangers we meet today,
Tomorrow become our friends.
And so, this chain of friendship,
Seems to have no end.

But the years go by, and the links are less,
As one by one, they slip away.
And we find that sorrow invades our life,
And takes away happiness.

The tie that binds our hearts in love,
Is broken and damaged in grief.
All that we have, of the times we shared,
Are memories, now bittersweet.

We long for the day when the links are restored,
And the chain is complete once again.
And earthly sorrows are vanished away
In that Land of Beginning Again.

The Bible tells us, we will know as we are known.
And we know that His Word is true.
We will find in Heaven, this friendship we shared,
So much sweeter has grown.

So, we will keep our memories close in our heart,
Till once again we meet.
And in Heaven we will find, this chain of friendship
Will be forever complete.

FRIENDS

If it were possible to go back in Time,
And freeze the years that seemed so fine.
I would go back the "Fifties" decade,
Happy years, when we were not afraid.
You could hitch a ride, or walk at night.
You seldom heard of a vengeful fight.
Most neighbors lived with an open door;
They helped each other with difficult chores.

Then the early "Sixties" was about the same.
Until the "Hippie Movement" and "Flower Children" came.
But we were young, and had many friends.
It seemed the "good times" would never end.
Then so quickly, the days and years were past.
But the friendships we made, continued to last.
Our children played, and we worked together,
Through days of sun, and winter weather.

Then the clock began to run so fast.
We found ourselves looking back at the past.
Our friends began to be sick and ill.
But the "Tie that Binds" held us still.
One by One, they slipped away,
And now, their grandchildren, we watch at play.
Old age and bad health is taking place,
Difficult times, and sorrows we face.

But the Truth that keeps us from being sad.
Are the beautiful memories of the good life we have had.
It is hard to watch our friends suffer, and leave;
But we have no time for our hearts to grieve.
Our wonderful memories, death cannot steal,
For the friendships we shared, grows even more real.
For Eternity waits, and soon we will meet.
And we will be friends forever, on the Golden Street.

Just For Smiles

A merry heart maketh a cheerful countenance.
Proverbs 15:13a

THE GOOD OLD "POOR" DAYS

A dollar for a candy bar, or perhaps a pack of gum,
Potato chips and Pepsi colas, add up to quite a sum.
When we were growing up, such luxuries were not there.
We never had a bag of chips, or popcorn popped with air.

We had Mary Janes, and BB bats, and penny bubble gum.
But to get a nickel candy bar, was rarely ever done.
We had no "spending" money, and seldom went to town.
There were no Malls, or Rec Halls, no MacDonalds were around.

We never saw a Game Arcade, no iPods, cell phones, or CDs.
We never heard of texting; of video games we had no need.
There were no DVDS, no Blue Ray games to play.
We seldom went to movies as we could not afford to pay.

Pizza was unheard of, computers weren't around.
Not many homes had telephones, and televisions, seldom found.
We listened to the radio, we read a lot of books.
There were no microwaves; Mom built a fire to cook.

The stove was not electric, Mom built a fire each day.
And after we brought the firewood in, we were allowed to play.
Central heat and air conditioning, we did not know about,
The heater in the living room warmed a small part of the house.

A bedroom of our own, we did not know could exist.
Brother slept with brother, and sister slept with sis.
Sometimes there were no inside bathrooms,
A galvanized tub was our bath.
The toilet was called the "outhouse"
And to go, you walked the path.

Our clothes were not the "brand" names,
Sometimes they were not new.
They were handed down from others,
But we put them to good use.

We went barefoot in the Summer and saved our shoes for school.
We really didn't mind, going barefoot was so cool.

We carried many buckets of water up the hill,
So, Mom could use the wash board in the tub that we would fill.
When Mother washed our clothes, she hung them on the line.
The only dryer that she had, was wind, and bright Sunshine.

Some places where we lived had no electric lights,
The oil lamp globes were washed each day,
So, we could see at night.
Ironing clothes was quite a feat, with flat irons on the stove.
You learned by touch, the length of time,
They reached the proper heat.

We didn't spend our evenings watching silly programs on TV;
We played outside with friends, till it was too dark to see.
We played "hide and seek" and "kick the can"
And "dodge ball" was our game.
We pitched horseshoes in the back yard
And a tree held our tire swing.
We played Monopoly, and board games,
And made our home-made kites.
Some kids were really lucky, for they possessed a bike.

We never went to Dairy Queen, TCBY did not exist,
We made "snow cream" when it snowed,
You don't know what you missed.
If all this to you seems boring, and you think our life was sad.
I wish you could be so lucky, to have the fun we had.

I AM NOT OLD

You look at me, and say, I'm old.
My hair is white, that once was gold.
My shoulders now are not so wide,
My steps are shorter in their stride.

My arms, their strength is lesser now,
A smaller load, my back will bow.
My eyes need help to see what's near;
A lot of sounds my ears don't hear.

But you are seeing just a shell.
The real me inside, is doing well.
You see what age can do in time,
But that's not me, I am really fine.

My inward man is young and strong.
What is really me, has nothing wrong.
So, when you think I am growing old,
The final story is not yet told.

The house in which the real me dwells
Is not my home, it is just a shell.
When my real life is just begun,
You will see,
I will be
Forever young.

HOME

When we reach the time of Old Age,
Sometimes we are left alone.
We are filled with a lonely feeling,
And our hearts are yearning for home.

But where is home now, we wonder,
Could we return to the days that are gone?
Where is the home that we cherished,
Where we would feel we belonged?

The house where we raised our family,
No longer would be a home.
For the children have gone their way now,
And we still would be alone.

So, the homesickness we feel is unending,
Nowhere do we feel content.
The years have passed so quickly,
And our days are nearly spent.

Our hearts are filled with such longing,
To see loved ones and friends we have known.
So, we hope, and dream for tomorrow,
When we will find,
HEAVEN IS HOME.

LETTER TO HEAVEN
Written for a special friend

I am putting our home on the market,
The house that was our home,
For if Home is where the Heart is,
Then our Home, is where you have gone.

If walls could talk, what a story
Our house would have to share;
Of all the loving and living we've done here,
Raising our family with care.

All the Christmases, birthdays, and dinners,
How the rooms with laughter rang.
And our hearts were so contented
As the children played and sang.

We had sickness, heartaches, and sorrows,
But always the Sun shone through,
And I knew I could face each tomorrow,
For I would face it with you.

Now I am packing to leave our home place,
And it is hard not to sit down and cry.
You always wanted me to be happy,
So, I know I have to try.

I'll move to another location
But each memory is packed with care.
And I will cherish, love, and remember,
Till our new home in Heaven, we share.

DESPAIR

The little fuzzy worm was filled with despair.
For nobody loved him, nobody cared.
When he came above ground to see the light of day,
Somebody always, kicked him away.

So, the little fuzzy worm said, "It's no use.
There is no point in trying, and that is not an excuse
Nobody wants me, it is plain to see,
I'm just an old worm, poor old me."

So, the little fuzzy worm went back into the ground,
Said, "Never again, will I be found.
Sunning myself on the grass so green."
So, he buried himself, to be nevermore seen.

In the hole in the ground, he became full of hate,
Said, "I am not coming out.
I am just going to wait."

But one day a fisherman dug a hole in the ground,
Said, "Come here boys, look what I found."
So, he took the little worm, which was much larger now,
Said, "If you want to catch a fish, let me show you how."

So, the little worm, who thought his life never counted,
Now hangs on the wall,
Inside a large fish, mounted.

THE HARRIED HOUSEWIFE'S DAY
Life in the Sixties

It is up at Six, with a bottle for baby,
Eggs to fry, no time for biscuits and gravy.
There is a lunch to pack, and get Daddy gone,
And now the morning has just begun.
There are dishes to wash, a formula to make,
A wash to put in, and beds to make.
Then when you think you might get through.
Up for his breakfast comes the toddler, age two.

An hour goes by, by the time he is fed,
And the baby of one month's face is getting red.
She is ready for a bottle, that is still on ice.
And she must have a bath, why can't she be quiet?
At last, she is fed, and burped, and dried.
But the wash load of clothes, is still inside.
By the time I get it put on the line,
The toddler of two, has started to whine.

Now he's had his lunch, and he is down for a spell,
And I think, at last, all is going well.
I start to vacuum, and the bathroom's to clean.
Now why on earth, did the phone have to ring?
Well, the floors are vacuumed, and the kitchen is mopped,
And right about now, I am ready to drop.
I make myself a cup of coffee, but before I can sip,
The baby starts again, having a fit.

Another bottle gone, now at last I can eat,
But no, number two, is up from his sleep.
So, I bring in the clothes, fold and put away.
Where on earth, has gone my day?
It is now four o'clock, and supper's to get,
But no, the little one is starting to fret.
She is yelling, and yelling, the pitch getting higher.
Thanks be to the one who invented pacifiers.

Now supper is ready, and Daddy is home.
"How, he says, has your day gone?"
The question with me, as I cry with despair,
Is not so much, how, as it is, where.
I sit down to supper, but it's never failed yet.
She is yelling for a bottle, and also, she's wet.
By the time she is down, my supper is cold.
No wonders Mothers get grey, before they get old.

The dishes are washed, and the kitchen is swept,
And now, at last, I will get some rest.
But no, someone's calling, and it is surely for me.
Well, three diapers later, now maybe T.V.
Now the toddler of two is bathed, and in bed.
But the face of the baby, is again getting red.
She must be starving, by the way she cries,
And I leave my easy chair with a sigh.

Now all is quiet, they are down for the night.
The house is a wreck, and I look a fright.
Oh well, why worry, tomorrow's another day,
So, I take a bath, and at last, hit the hay.
Now I may complain, but it's the life that I chose.
And though it isn't a bed of roses.
Though I get so tired, still I wouldn't trade.
My two little ones, for anything made.

NO REGRETS

We had a ride on Life's Ferris Wheel
We rode all the way to the top,
And for a brief span of time, the world was ours,
As the wheel, came to a stop.

We saw life from a different view,
In a world that was all our own.
High above the rest, we were so in love,
And happy, just me and you.

Then we heard the wheel turn,
As it began to descend.
And even more quickly, than it had begun,
Our ride had come to an end.

As we left the wheel, and walked away,
I looked back, with a bittersweet pain.
For the time we had, and the love we shared,
In my heart, will always remain.

What a joy it has been with you at my side,
And even if I am left alone.
Though my heart may break, and tears may fall,
I still wouldn't have missed the ride.

THE MIGHTY TOOTH

When we consider the parts of the body,
The tooth seems very small.
Compared to the arms and the legs,
It hardly measures at all.

When a young baby is teething,
There are many nights of tears,
But the family is aglow with wonder
When the first small tooth appears.

They think it is so wonderful,
And everyone they meet,
They cannot wait to show them,
Their baby now has teeth.

The tooth alone is defenseless,
Sometimes it is removed with a blow,
But if it becomes infected,
Its mighty strength it will show.

A full-grown man is helpless,
If the tooth for attention cries,
He will find he's no match for its power;
The tooth's importance is magnified.

He will walk the floor at midnight,
And cry and beg for relief.
Learning his lesson the hard way:
The importance of tiny teeth.

THE GOLDEN YEARS

If the Sun hits my head, I get a migraine;
If I lift the least load, I get a pain.
The corners of my mouth have lines that droop,
My clothes don't fit, cause my shoulders stoop.
My hair turns grey, and starts to fall out,
My legs have bad veins, and my back goes out.
If I sleep on my back, I know I will snore,
If I sleep on my side, my arm gets sore.

When eating late, all the food I question,
Will it keep me awake with indigestion?
Under my eyes, there are always bags,
And my once trim figure, now sadly sags.
The strength in my hand is not very strong,
My days are short, and my nights are long.
My skin that once, was smooth as down,
Is covered now with spots of brown.

Old age spots are what they are.
The beauty of youth, they certainly mar.
My face that once was smooth and fine
Is etched deep now, with lines of Time.

The problems, worries, and life's cares
My brow has wrinkled, that once was fair.
Now my vision has become blurred,
And I was told another fact,
My glasses don't need changing,
It's because of cataracts.

When we were young we all were told
That our older years, were days of gold.
I'm here to say, it is all a myth.
The Golden Years do not exist.

NO USE TO COMPLAIN

If you think that Life's not fair
That you are not receiving your rightful share.
No use to complain.
Because the world doesn't care.

If you don't get what you think you are due,
And only the bad is handed to you.
If the rains come down, and the sun doesn't shine,
You can't change the weather, so no use to whine.

If all you have are aches and pains,
No one cares, so why complain?
Some people think it is what you deserve,
Most aren't listening,
You aren't even heard.

No use to complain as we go along,
So, we may as well smile, and have a song.
When people ask, "How are you today?"
They don't really care,
So just say, "Okay."

OUR CONSCIENCE

It is true we all have a conscience
Which no one has ever seen.
The conscience does its best work,
Always behind the scene.

When we lash out with words of anger,
Or wrongly place the blame.
Immediately our conscience goes to work,
Filling our hearts with shame.

When we decide to do wrong,
As soon as the act is done,
Our conscience speaks to our heart,
And takes away all the fun.

If we ignore our conscience continually
And listen not, when it speaks.
We will find its strength to control us,
Each time, becoming more weak.

Though we cannot see our conscience
It is a gift from above,
It is a tool God uses
To guide us with care, and with love.

So, listen when your conscience tells you,
You have chosen the wrong way to go.
If you heed its voice of warning,
You'll be spared much hurt, and much woe.

THE WHALE'S TALE

Every day I eat what passes through these mighty flowing waters,
But I swallowed one today, and I think, I hadn't oughta.
I eat most anything but today was quite a scare;
I swallowed this man, Jonah, before I even knew he was there.

As I swim these waters daily eating everything without question.
But since I swallowed this man called Jonah,
I've had a bad case of indigestion.
It has been three days now, and I am really hurting more.
I think I am about ready to throw him up along the shore.

From now on, I'll only feed on fishes, clams,
With or without shells.
But I hope I never swallow a man,
Running from God, trying to rebel.

SKOOLIES

For my son, David, and his new adventure.

Once there was a band of people,
Across the land they roamed.
Wherever the nighttime found them,
That's where they called their home.

They were known as gypsies; some said they were all fools.
But now a new bunch travel in buses once used by schools.

The gypsies went in horse-drawn wagons,
Fueled by horses eating grass.
What would they think of Skoolies –
And what they pay for gas?

THE NIGHT BEFORE WEIGHT WATCHERS

'Twas the night before Weight Watchers
And all through the house,
My stomach was squeaking,
Like a hungry mouse.

The kitchen was scrubbed and cleaned with care,
Not a trace of food was seen anywhere.
The children were sleeping, and so was my spouse;
But still my stomach squeaked like a mouse.

When out in the kitchen I found myself,
Grabbing food from the cabinets and shelf.
When my husband appeared, said, "What is the matter,
And what are you doing with that ham on that platter?"

He grabbed the plate, put it back on the shelf,
Shook me so soundly, said, "Get hold of yourself.
Go back to bed, and go back to sleep,
And tomorrow you will be glad, you didn't cheat."

As I put down the platter, and was turning around,
I found my stomach, not making a sound.
It was all in my head, I found after all,
My mind, not my stomach, was making me fall.

So back to the bedroom, I hastily sped,
Threw back the covers and jumped into bed.
But I said to myself, as I drifted to sleep;
"Don't count the lamb chops, just count the sheep."

FIFTY YEARS TOGETHER

Old age is golden, the young always say,
But if the later years are golden,
there is a price to pay.
In purest form, the gold is weak,
it has not strength to stand,
It goes thru fiery furnaces
to make a wedding band.

And it is true in married life,
There are hardships to go through.
The little daily triumphs,
are what prove a love is true.

Gold alone, is weak, it has to be infused,
With other precious metals,
to be strong enough to use.

Fifty years of marriage, is a milestone so we are told,
We say, "a special anniversary,
So special it is gold."

Fifty years, a half century, seems eons to the young,
But it was only yesterday, it seems,
Our journey was begun.

If I could turn Time's Clock back
And live my life anew.
And choose my life's companion,
My choice would still be you.

THE MIRROR

One day I looked in the mirror
And said, "Who is this I see?
With wrinkled skin and greying hair,
I know this is not me!"

The person in the mirror
Shows one with much more weight.
She has lines around her mouth,
This is not my face.

I'm taking this mirror back to the store,
And ask them "What's the matter?"
It shows someone who I don't know,
This person is much fatter.

Maybe the lighting is causing this,
Maybe natural light would help.
Surely something has to give...
I don't recognize myself.

THE OPTIMIST AND THE PESSIMIST

It's a beautiful day, said the optimist,
The sun is shining so bright,
But I see a cloud in the West, said the pessimist,
It will probably rain before night.

Let's take a walk, said the optimist,
The fresh air will do us good.
But I just had my hair done, said the pessimist
I would have to wear a hood.

Look at the beautiful flowers, said the optimist
They fill your heart with a song,
Yes, said the pessimist,
But the blooms don't last very long.

The future looks bright, said the optimist,
We have nothing to fear or dread.
The pessimist answered sadly,
Tomorrow, we may all be dead.

MAMA'S COFFEEPOT

Mama's old coffee pot set back on the shelf
In the dust of years gone by,
No use to put it in the Yard Sale,
For who would even buy?

Everyone wants the new style now
Equipped with timers, and such,
They are made of glass and plastic,
But they give the modern touch.

One day someone asked for the old coffee pot,
And as I brought it down from the shelf,
A flood of memories swept over me,
And I could hear Dad, himself.

I could see him at the kitchen table
In his chair, where he always sat,
Asking the same question each morning,
"Mama, is the coffee ready yet?"

Memories of my childhood days
Flooded my heart with such pain,
And I was filled with such longing,
To see Mama and Daddy again.

They have no use where they are now,
For the old coffee pot, left below,
They are drinking from eternal fountains,
From the River of Life's crystal flow.

MEMORIES

Standing in line at the Grocery Store,
My mind went back to the days of yore.
A young Mother and baby, in front of the line
Made me flash back, to an earlier time.

Seems just a few days ago, I saw myself
Taking baby food from the grocery shelf.
That was back in an earlier time.
When a jar of baby food, cost only a dime.

The baby in line was a beautiful boy
And I could remember the feelings of joy.
I was the young mother with the wonderful son,
Seems just a short while ago, that he was one.

Then I went to the store with two by my side,
For a darling girl, now brought us such pride.
I remember the feelings when people would smile,
And remark, "How sweet," and admire each child.

Now, I am the one who remembers the past,
And I know all too well, childhood doesn't last.
For my children are grown and are parents as well.
Now it's grandchildren, that makes my heart swell.

To the young mother in line at the grocery store,
Make each moment count with this child you adore.
Treasure each day, and put memories away
To brighten your heart, as mine is today.

LIFE HAS CHANGES

An Indian Tribe had settled on the Plain
They decided they would never move again.
They said, "We are happy, we like it here.
There are plenty of buffalo and a lot of deer."

One day the Chief called a meeting of the Clan,
He said, "Let me tell you about my plan.
I think it's time to move, and I think what is best,
We should pack up, and head for the West."

Some left the meeting, and some looked around
Some stood still, with their eyes to the ground.
They said, "We don't think it's time, and in our belief,
You can't make us go, even though you are Chief."

"Our Village still has room to grow,
And we don't understand why you think we should go.
We have empty wigwams, and there's lots of space,
We're not leaving this wonderful place."

The Chief said, "You know I am not a dictator,
But my decision is now, and not later.
If you want to follow me, as your elected Chief,
Be ready to go to this new land we will seek."

Most of the Tribe agreed to head for the West,
For they trusted their Chief to know what was best.
But some stayed back on the lush green Plain,
Where the tall grass flourished with abundant rain.

A year went by, and the Plain grew dry,
Not one drop of water fell from the sky.
The grass all died, and the deer were gone,
And the Indians who stayed,
Said, "What have we done?"

But the Chief and his followers were happy out West,
He had done what his conscience had told him was best.
They built new Villages, and the Tribe was at peace,
Their needs were all met, and they greatly increased.

The moral of the story is plain to see,
Too set in our ways, sometimes we can be.
Changes in our lives, are usually for our good.
Even when the reason
Is not always understood.

THE OLD HOME PLACE

This old house has been so good.
It is more than mortar, brick, and wood,
It's been our haven, it's been our home,
And we will miss it, when it is gone.

For nearly a century this house has been,
It has sheltered families and welcomed friends.
It has heard many voices, that now are quiet,
It's heard many "Good Mornings"
And many "Good Nights."

It may be old, and weathered with time,
But it's had much care, and still looks fine.
Many times, on a cold winter night,
We have returned to its warmth, and light.

It has sheltered us from the cold and snow,
Its walls have protected when strong winds did blow.
Its roof has kept off sun, and rain,
Many morning lights have graced the windowpanes.

So, when we return to where the house stood,
We'll say, "Old house, you were very good,
You were our haven, you were our home,
And we will miss you, when you are gone."

THE PIANO TEACHER

To teach the art of music
Is like throwing pebbles in a pond,
The ripples go and go,
And reach to lands beyond.

Music is a gift,
And when one attains the art,
It stays with him throughout his life,
And always warms his heart.

To instill in others the gift of music
Is casting bread upon the waters,
For as they go thru life,
They bless so many others.

The student you teach today,
Tomorrow another will bless
With the power of wonderful music
That brings such happiness.

If you teach for many years,
You may never meet the ones,
Who have been blessed by the seeds you've sown,
In teaching the little ones.

It must be a wonderful feeling
To know you have been a part,
In sharing the gift of music,
And lifting so many hearts.

A LASTING LOVE

The sparkle in her eye is dimmed
When clouded by cataracts.
Her figure that once was firm and trim,
Now wears a larger pair of slacks.

His shoulders that were strong and straight,
Now stoop with years of work and aches.
Where once his hair was thick and fine,
Has fallen out, his bald head shines.

Their hearing fades, their eyesight dims,
But love remains the same as when;
They had their youthful days of fun,
When first, they two, became as one.

For time and years cannot erase,
A life of love preserved by Grace.
And though the outward flesh has changed,
The love within their heart remains.

Two people will not always agree;
And sometimes the tempers flared,
But they worked out their problems,
Because they knew, how much in their hearts they cared.

A lifetime of memories and happiness known,
Love in old age, much sweeter has grown.
When Death comes to part them from this life so brief;
The joys love brought, will overshadow the grief.

CHRIST IN THE CLASSROOM

Christ is unwelcome in the classroom today;
He is completely ignored, they don't even pray.
He is not acknowledged in our public schools,
They do as they please and make their own rules.
Though He is not acknowledged, He is still there,
For we know that God is everywhere.
The students sit at desks made of wood.
Wood from trees God created, and even called good.

The air they breathe and the water they drink,
Where does it come from, they don't stop to think
They take all of God's goodness, and all He has wrought.
Giving glory to self, and of God they think naught.

Man is sufficient within himself they say,
To decide how to live, to work, and to play.
We need not a Sovereign over us to rule,
We will decide what is taught in our schools.
We'll take the credit for everyone knows,
Higher education is what makes our world go,
So, they fill our minds with figures and facts.
Never thinking of God, or His mighty acts.

They seek for more knowledge year after year
Not realizing, wisdom begins with Godly fear.
Science, evolution, enlightening the mind,
Will all come to naught, one day they will find.
Man left to himself becomes a fool,
No matter how brilliant the professors in school.

When we leave God out, and lean on man's arm,
We are cheating our children and doing them harm.
We long for the day when our schools once again,
Acknowledge the Saviour and point children to Him.
Our children wouldn't live under false hope and gloom.
If Christ would be welcomed to every classroom.

THE LIFE OF A BIRD

The male bird flits and flies all around,
Here and there, all around the town,
While Mama Bird sits on the nest,
He says, "All you do, is rest."

"Here I am running here and there,
Hunting straw and leaves for the nest so bare.
I'm bringing it in, running off my legs,
While all you do, is sit on the eggs."

The mama bird sits still and quiet,
Never leaving the nest, day, or night.
While daddy bird thinks he's big stuff,
Bringing to the nest a little fluff.

One day, mama says, "You sit down,
Let me fly all over this town,
You've seen all the places and been everywhere,
While I've been sitting, on the nest right here."

So, daddy bird gets on the nest,
Says, "All she does is sit and rest."
But soon he's restless and wants to fly,
He says, "I'm so bored, I think I'll die."

So, mama bird comes back, and takes her place,
While he has to admit, he's a little red faced.
He says, "You are the one with the most to do.
Never again, will I envy you."

Tributes & Remembrances
of Some Who Have Encouraged Me, and Brightened My Day

Be thou an example of the believers,
in word, in conversation, in charity, in spirit, in faith, in purity.
1 Timothy 4:12b

MAMA'S ROCKING CHAIR

For my dear friend and neighbor, Dot Harris.

We went to visit Mama at the Nursing Home today,
They told us we could take her rocking chair away.
She now needs a chair with wheels,
To help her get around, and to go for her meals.

We had to put Mama in the Nursing Home
When it wasn't safe to leave her alone.
She seems happy and she gets good care;
But it was hard to take away her rocking chair.

Mama loved her chair, but even when she would sit,
Those little hands were busy, with something to sew or knit.
Mama worked hard, she helped everyone she knew,
And when she came home from her outside job
There was still a lot of work to do.

She was picking grapes for making jam,
And her church knew, if they called on her,
She would say, "Here I am."

Countless loaves of homemade bread
She gave away to friends,
Jams and jellies she would share;
Her generosity had no end.

Now those little hands that worked so hard
Are gnarled and knotted with life's cares,
We still see them gently folded,
Rocking in her chair.

Sometimes she has a faraway look in her eyes;
We know she sees what we can't see.
She sees Daddy waiting for her
In their new home in heaven's skies.

AS YOU RETIRE

For Pastor Thomas Pierce and his wife, Barbara.

Remembering the years when you and Barbara first came,
Such happy times, so many faces and names.
We were all so happy to have you on board,
To preach all the truths of our wonderful Lord.
When Barbara played the organ and we heard her sweet voice,
We knew God had sent us His perfect choice.

Every milestone, every soul saved,
Every tear that was shed as some went to the grave.
Every happy time, every shared meal,
Every sermon explaining God's truth so real.

Time and tide wait for no man, they say;
We all have dreaded your Retirement Day.
Time has endeared us as family and friends,
Retirement won't mean your ministry ends.

Infants and children, you've watched as they grew,
Nurtured in love by Barbara and you.
Investing in us, you have given so much;
You have pastored and loved us, with a true shepherd's touch.

Realizing now what a treasure we've had,
Makes your retirement so very sad.
Richer we are for all you have given,
Your final reward will be given in Heaven.

Eternity will reveal what has been wrought,
Through the sermons you've preached and lessons you've taught.
You have earned your retirement,
Though we know your life will still preach,
As God's love you will show to all those you meet.
When life here is over, and in Heaven we greet,
We will rejoice together on the golden streets.

THIS I KNOW

In memory of my mother, Thelma Todd,
who died of ALS on July 1, 1998.

The doctors say I have ALS and there is nothing they can do.
But there are other words for ALS that I have found to be true.
The other ALS I met early in my life,
It was A LOVING SAVIOUR, who bought me with a price.

So, ALS may rob my health, and leave my muscles weak,
But A LOVING SAVIOUR that I serve, will keep my heart in peace.
The ALS my body has brings fear and deep distress,
But A LOVING SAVIOUR stays close by, to comfort and to bless.

I do not know what lies ahead, what this ALS will do.
I trust A LOVING SAVIOUR, and He will see me through.
So, when this disease of ALS has wracked and ruined my frame;
I'll claim A LOVING SAVIOUR'S promise and call upon His name.

Life at its best, is very brief, and filled with pain and grief.
But Heaven waits for me, I know,
When this mortal life shall cease.

WHEN BILLY REACHED HOME

For Evangelist Billy Kelly.

The conversation in Heaven
Was an exciting and thrilling one,
For it was noised abroad
That "Billy" was coming home.

Dr. Sightly and Dr. Kanoy hurried to the Gate,
That is where they two would wait.
They said, "Let's get his baby boy
And stand him by the Throne,
For we know that is the first place
Billy will go on his own."

So, the angels came at God's bidding
As He sent them down to earth,
To transport Billy to his new home,
Prepared since his "new birth."

Billy knew it was time for his leaving
And he knew that Dot and his family would sorrow.
But He also knew that very soon,
Each of them would follow.

I think the angels stood amazed
As they heard someone enter with quite a new phrase.
"It's Jubilee Time!" they heard him say,
As Billy entered the Land of Eternal Day.

He sang so often, no stranger he'd be
For he had many friends waiting to see.
Now he is at home, and we will miss him here.
He is with his Saviour, Whom he loved so dear.

A PICTURE OF FAITH

For good friends Martin and Ann Hykin.

When Martin comes through the sanctuary door
We know what a blessing we have in store.
He shakes each hand and greets each one;
He likes to tease and have his fun.
He carefully looks at every pew
And if he finds someone who is new,
He takes special time to welcome them
And tell them he hopes they will come again.

He remembers names, and never forgets;
I don't think a stranger he has ever met.
But the past few Sundays we missed his face,
For no one in church can take Martin's place.
Pastor asks when the service is over for the day,
"Does anyone else have something to say?"
All eyes turn to Martin, waiting to hear
His words of encouragement, hope and cheer.

We can't think of Martin without thinking of Ann,
For she lifts us up, just like Martin can.
A more willing worker you will never find,
When Martin found Ann, he found a gold mine!

They say the ones with the hardest tests
Are the ones whom God loves the best.
Martin and Ann have passed the grade,
Two finer Christians have never been made.
So, thanks, Martin and Ann, for letting us see
What a true child of God is supposed to be.

We don't understand all you have had to endure,
But you are an example of God's love, true and pure.
You have honored God and have lived so true,
We are asking the Father for complete healing for you.

GOOD AND FAITHFUL SERVANT
Tribute to Pastor Roy Rector.

When God sent the angels for Roy
He said, "Bring him home with much care,
But leave behind the walker and canes,
And he won't ever need the wheelchair."

For the body that I have waiting
Will never tire or grow old.
The new legs and feet prepared for him
Will run on streets of gold.

His new lungs will be filled
With ethereal heavenly air
And though there will never be night here,
He won't have to recline in a chair.

The weary stoop from his shoulders
Will be replaced with muscles strong.
And he will walk through the hills of Heaven
As he did in the mountains, when young.

When I saved Roy, I decided
To try him with sickness and pain,
But each time the affliction was greater,
It seemed the more grace he gained.

Now his sufferings and trials are over
And eternal victories he has won.
My welcoming words await him –
"Good and faithful servant,
Well done!"

MY TRIBUTE

To my friend, Dr. Ralph Sexton, Sr.

I think I know how the disciples felt
On the Mount of Transfiguration,
For it has been my privilege and joy
To observe a saint in the making.

For many years I have witnessed a life
That was lived so true, without malice or strife.
I never saw him angry or heard him be unkind,
I never saw him judge another, or any fault to find.

I know what kept him tender,
It was the time he spent on his knees.
And if one fell along life's way,
He'd say, "But for God's grace, it could be me."

I never saw him without his Bible very near,
He loved God's Word supremely; to him it was most dear.
He had a vast knowledge of the Word,
With scholars he could place.
But he kept the gospel message simple –
So even a child could understand grace.

No respecter of persons could he ever be called,
The richest to the poorest, he witnessed to them all.
He spoke God's word with boldness, but love was on his face.
And you didn't have to know him long
To sense the presence of God's grace.

A spiritual giant has been taken from us,
And no one will take his place.
Though God will always have a witness
To tell the world of His grace.

But this gentle mountain man
Who could have had earth's fame,
Graced our life with his presence,
And we will never be the same.

When the angels came for his crossing
I am sure they were specifically told,
What a valiant soldier and warrior
They were bringing to the City of Gold.

He loved to preach about Heaven,
And now he has found it all true.
The Saviour he loved, and served with such faith
Was there to welcome and greet him,
As he entered the beautiful gate.

THE CHRISTIAN'S TEST

In honor of our friend, Frank Duckett.

When I was young, and lean, and tall
I had no worries, or cares at all.
My hands were able, my back was strong,
I could work, and labor, all day long.

My legs were strong, I could run with the best,
Never thinking once of stopping to rest.
My arms would wield a hammer or hug my wife.
I was perfectly content with my lot in life.

But one day, I heard a strange request,
"Would you be willing to take a test?
I have watched your life, and you have lived so true,
That is why in My wisdom, I have chosen you."

I said, "I will try, but I don't know
How far in this test I am willing to go
He said, "Oh, don't worry, I will see you through.
There will never be a moment, I am not with you."

He said, "There will be times you will want to give up,
You will say, 'Please take away this bitter cup.
This isn't fair, it is too much to ask,
I can't finish this awful task.'

'You know a man wants to be strong
Not sit in a chair all the day long.
You know it is our nature to work and to lead,
Not depend on others, for our every need.'"

He said, "When you were looking for a partner in life,
I chose for you a very special wife,
I knew she was the one that you could depend
To be faithful and help to the very end."

He said, "My child, I can already tell
In this awful trial, you will surely excel.
You have kept a beautiful smile on your face,
You are showing the world, the power of Grace.

"You are a true witness of what I can do,
You have allowed Me, to work through you.
Though your strength is gone, you have done so well.
For this outward body, is just a shell.

"The real you inside is young and strong.
The real man inside, has nothing wrong.
I have made others to see,
When they look on your face,
The Christ-like image,
A picture of Grace."

A PARADE OF MEMORIES

For Pastor Ralph Sexton, Jr. on his retirement.

I see a parade, what a grand array;
It's a special salute called Pastor Ralph's Day.
No way you can see to the end of the line,
This parade encompasses nearly fifty years in time.

As each one passes before you, look back in your mind.
So many memories, I am sure you will find.

The first ones to come are a noisy group.
No wonder, it is those who were teens,
When you had the youth.
Halfway back a large banner unfurls,
"We represent Muzette's Proverbs 31 Girls!"

Then here comes a crowd, must be a mile long,
They come from miles away; who makes up this throng?
What is that they are holding?
It's a piece of a tent,
Held by some you preached to,
And caused to repent.

They are only a portion of souls that you reached
As you traveled long miles, and the Gospel you preached.
You will never know how many were won,
As you showed them salvation
Through Jesus, God's only Son.

The next group is from churches; what a long line —
Where you have held revivals time after time.
Thanking you for encouraging their ministries too,
Joining the parade to give honor to you.

Then here comes a group, some walking with canes;
They were still young adults when as "Pastor" you came.
You preached to their children; you counseled and led;
You shared in their sorrows when they buried their dead.
Now their grandchildren sit in the same place,
While you still proclaim God's message of Grace.

Another crowd now joins the parade;
They have heard the Gospel by means of air waves.
You faithfully preached, to God's Word you stayed true.
Eternity will reveal what God has wrought through you.

So many memories and stories to tell,
You've been a true friend and as Pastor, excelled.
So today, Pastor Ralph, we give honor to you.
Enjoy your retirement, though we know you aren't through.

Take time to relax,
Enjoy your garden and birds.
We know you will still be busy
Sharing God's Word.

TO THE PREACHER

For my friend, Dr. Ralph Sexton, Sr.

When I was just a teen, I had a friend
Who took me to a church in Asheville's West End.
It was not a lovely place; to me it was a shock.
There was no carpet on the floor,
And the pews were hard as rock.

The lighting there was poor; there was no central heat.
In wintertime there was a rush by the stove to get a seat.
The altar was made of stone and the pulpit stand was rough,
The Sunday School was all together
And to hear was sometimes tough.

But in this crude rough building, in the pulpit was a gem;
I had heard a lot of preachers, but never one like him.
Since childhood I had been in Sunday School,
But the sermons in this church
Were more than just the Golden Rule.

Then as the years went by and the congregation grew
We bought another church with a lot better pews.
But the message from the pulpit never varied, never changed.
It was always what we needed,
Like gardens need the rain.

Every Sunday was a treat, which we knew would never fail;
Something fresh and needed from God's Word would be revealed.
There were promises reminded and the Word was made so plain,
To hear such preaching,
I would always come again.

Then as the years went by, the messages group deeper;
I know the Preacher was always in God's keeping.
He has taught me more than I ever could contain;
Each time the message always
Makes a new truth plain.

Then I married and my husband and my children
Were blessed as I had been
To know such a prophet for a pastor and a friend.
Through the years so many have been blessed
By this man's preaching,
And today as God is blessing, there are more that he is reaching.

Through the printed page and air waves
So many now can hear
And be blessed by the message
That brings God's plan so clear.

He has stayed on course and has been true to the Word.
We know that in Heaven he will receive his reward.

THE OLD SHOE'S STORY
A Tribute to Pastors

While volunteering in the thrift shop one day,
I saw a pair of shoes, someone had given away.
They thought some needy one the shoes could wear;
They were well worn, the soles almost bare.
I picked up the shoes to put on display,
And I wondered who had thrown them away.
The shoes seemed to have a soul, and a way;
I almost thought I could hear them say.

"I was privileged to cover the feet of a man,
Who walked with God and was part of His plan.
He was a preacher, a proclaimer of God's Word divine.
And when he wore me, he always saw that I shined.
I saw many places travelling on his feet.
From the pulpit where he brought messages so sweet.
Sometimes in the midnight, again we would leave
To go to a home where some poor soul grieved.

"Many times, we walked the hospital halls
As he faithfully visited and made his calls.
To Nursing Homes where the elderly dwell,
He would cheer and encourage them
With hope and glad tidings, he came to tell.
Many times, in the night these shoes he'd put on,
As he answered the door, where some needy had come.
Sometimes they needed help, and sometimes prayer;
But he'd put on these shoes, and their burdens he'd share.

"He would wear me to weddings and to occasions of joy,
Sometimes to dedicate a new baby girl, or boy.
Sometimes I'd get wet in the Baptismal Pool,
Sometimes we'd go to baccalaureate service at school.
You see I really have a story to tell;
For I've been many places and have been worn so well.

"But now I am worn and shabby, and old;
And I have been thrown out, to be secondhand sold.
But the reason I tell you all these things in my chatter;
Is the One who wore me, is the one who matters.

"You see, like me, he is now older and worn.
And we've walked together, through so many storms.
I'm just a shoe, I can be replaced, or resold.
But he is God's creation, a never dying soul.
He has given his life for his fellow man, and for God;
And I am proud to have been there, his feet to shod.

"I know I am old and worn with Time,
But I can still be used, though sold for a dime.
I can warm someone's feet, keep them dry all day,
So, I am glad to be here, and not thrown away.

"I know the dear one who wore me so long,
Though he is old, he still has a song.
He still is helping his fellow man;
He still is a part of God's wonderful plan."

I am glad people are not like old shoes,
Which are thrown away when no longer use.
But down to old age, God promises to bless;
And use men and women, till He calls them to rest.

A LIFE WELL LIVED

For beloved family physician, Dr. William R. Snoddy, on his retirement.

Enter the grandstand, Dr. Snoddy, get ready to view
This parade today is in honor of you.

No way you can see the end of the line;
This parade encompasses more than forty years' time.

As these patients pass before you, look back in your mind.
So many memories I know you will find.

Some were very young when they first came;
Now they are old, some walking with canes.

Some when they came, were gravely ill,
But through your expertise they're enjoying life still.

The line would be longer, but some were so ill
Their health was too weak for mortal man's pills.

You came to work daily not thinking of self,
Facing all day those who needed help.

Not a very cheerful job, but you kept a smile on your face;
What patients found in your office was compassion and grace.

Some weren't very ill; they just needed care,
A listening ear for their problems to share.

As you view the parade, I hope you are aware
Of the impact you've made as your knowledge you shared.

So, enjoy your retirement; you have accomplished so much.
God has given much healing through your tender touch.

MY BROTHER BILLY

A tribute from Rev. Charles Worley, for his brother, Billy.

I have many childhood memories of the North Carolina hills;
One thing that made them happy was my older brother, Bill.

But one thing that bothered me I never quite could see,
When Daddy needed help, he'd choose Billy over me.

I used to get so mad when dad would say, "Billy, now let's go."
I wanted so to be a part; this really hurt me so.

I'd say, "Let me go, don't leave me here,"
But off they'd go, and not look back to see my childish tears.

I thought that Billy got to be a part; that Daddy loved him more.
But now I know that wasn't true; he just needed help with chores.

Then Daddy died, and Mama too; left Billy here with me.
And we loved each other dearly; we were brothers, don't you see?

Now once again, I feel alone; for our Heavenly Father did it too.
Said, "Billy, come, I need you now, but Charles' work's not through."

Once again, I am left; Billy got to go ahead.
But I know he's made it safely home; and I'll follow with no dread.

Billy, once again, you left me; you were first to make it home.
I have my Elder Brother, Jesus, with me now,
I'm not really left alone.

Billy and Charles were reunited on June 19, 2022,
when Charlie made it home.

MY DADDY

Written by our daughter, Sheila Alewine, for Robert's birthday (1992)

My Daddy is a special guy, I think you will agree.
He's always been so faithful to take good care of me.
I have a lot of memories of things that he has done,
Of ways he's sacrificed for his daughter, wife, and son.

I often see my Daddy hoeing a straight row
As Mom and I sit holding a stick tied to a rope.
I see my Daddy mowing our yard which was quite wide
And if I'd had to mow it, I think I would have died!

I see my Daddy leaving for work so late at night,
He stood out on the "catwalk" while I slept so tight.
I see my Daddy playing with a train that Santa brought,
My crew-cut brother helping with what Daddy really bought.

I see my Daddy standing in tall and itchy corn
Shucking as he picked it with hands so callous worn.
I see my Daddy picking beans from rows so straight;
And play time was over, for the beans we had to break.

I see my Daddy walking his daughter down the aisle,
And wedding photos tell it; he really didn't smile.
I see my Daddy holding his first grandchild so sweet,
Baby giggles warm his heart as he tickles little feet.

I see my Daddy crying, this time in a chapel pew;
He mourns the unexpected loss of a friend who was so true.
I've seen my Daddy lots of ways, both happy, sad, and blue;
It makes me realize that dads have feelings too.

You see my Daddy's special; he wears a lot of hats.
He's a father, son, friend, and spouse, and even more than that.
Though times may change around us and events reshape the world
He will always be my Daddy and I'll be his little girl.